16.95

MW01493458

THE COPS ARE ROBBERS

THE COPS ARE ROBBERS

A CONVICTED COP'S
TRUE STORY OF
POLICE CORRUPTION

GERALD W. CLEMENTE
with KEVIN STEVENS

QUINLAN PRESS
Boston

Library of Congress Cataloging-in-Publication Data

Clemente, Gerald W.
  The cops are robbers.

  1. Clemente, Gerald W. 2. Bank robberies—Massa-
chusetts—Medford. 3. Depositors Trust Company (Med-
ford, Mass.) 4. Brigands and robbers—Massachusetts—
Medford—Biography. I. Stevens, Kevin. II. Title.
HV6653.C44A3 1987   364.1'552'0924 [B] 86-43247
ISBN 0-933341-70-9

Printed in the United States of America
April 1987

To my wife, Mary, who has stood by me faithfully through good times and bad.

G.W.C.

We would like to thank the following people for their help: Henry Quinlan, for making the book possible; Mary and Barry Clemente, for providing research material and information; Sandy Bielawa, for her editorial expertise; Dennis Campbell, for his advice; George Bailey, for his knowledge of Medford; and Janice Stevens, for her support and encouragement.

All of the events described in this book actually took place. Some names, dates and locations have been changed to protect the privacy of real persons.

CONTENTS

Prologue

"Shit, only sixty grand."

Bucky Barrett stood away from the safe and wiped his forehead with the sleeve of his sweatshirt. His face glistened with sweat. His eyebrows were powdered with dust. Charley, Joe Bangs and I stopped what we were doing and looked at him.

"You're kidding," I said.

He reached into the safe, pulled out a bundle of twenties, and ruffled it with his thumb.

"Sixty bundles, a thousand in each. It's printed on the bands. The numbers don't lie, pal."

"Fuck this," Bangs said. *"Fuck this."*

Sixty grand. Ten thousand each. I steadied myself against the safe. In the big mirror at the end of the vault I could see the four of us reflected in the yellow rays of the droplight. The scene was bizarre: each of us wore a nylon stocking stretched over our hair, a dark long-sleeved shirt and a pair of white gloves, so that we looked like cartoon characters. But we had to take every precaution—Bucky had said the authorities could trace fingerprints, hair or even scraped skin.

"Damn!"

I banged the safe with my fist. All that work, all that planning, all that danger—and only ten thousand lousy bucks apiece. My throat was clogged with dust and my ears were still ringing with the sounds of dynamite blasting and drills spinning. I thought about everything I had at stake. I was a police officer with over twenty years experience. Now a captain, I had just come off duty as night-watch commander of the Metropolitan District Commission police, the force that patrols Boston's parks and parkways—and here I was robbing a bank in Medford, my hometown. Ten grand did not go very far towards justifying the risks.

Bangs turned back to the safety deposit boxes with his hammer and chisel. Charley stood with his bodybuilder's arms out from his side, his mouth open, his shirt caked with dirt. Like me, he was exhausted. Bucky started kicking the duffel bags and swearing.

"What kind of fucking operation is this, anyway? You drag me and Charley into this place, you get us into this operation up to our necks, and all there is is a measly sixty grand? What a waste of time, what a fucking waste of time!"

"Take it easy, Bucky," I said.

"Don't tell me to fucking take it easy. You guys are the cops, you're supposed to know these things. Doherty said there'd be a million bucks in this safe."

"So Doherty was wrong."

"Damn right he was wrong, damn right..."

Now Charley started swearing too, waving his arms in my face. Joe's hammer and chisel echoed in the vault. I felt lightheaded. The torches had eaten up the oxygen and turned the vault into a furnace. I was hot and edgy and claustrophobic. The last thing I needed was this aggravation. How had Tommy gone wrong?

"What the hell's going on down there?"

Brother O'Leary yelled down at us from his lookout post above the vault. His head appeared in the hole we had blasted through eighteen inches of steel-reinforced concrete.

"We're getting the fuck out of here, that's what's going on," Barrett shouted, "this whole thing is a fiasco."

"Hold on now, Bucky..."

"Cops," he fumed, "I should have known better than to think that cops would know what was going down."

By now Bangs had chiseled the hinges off a couple of deposit boxes and pried them open with a screwdriver so that each

box door swung open on the tongue of its lock. He dumped
some papers on the floor and stuffed money into his pants.

"C'mon Joe," Bucky said, "stop wasting your time. You
won't find nothing in there."

"You call this nothing?" Bangs said, waving some bills.

"Small change. If there ain't nothing in the safe there ain't
nothing anywhere."

Brother's head reappeared above.

"Hey Jerry, Tommy's on the radio. Wants to talk."

We all went quiet as Brother handed me the walkie-talkie.
Tommy Doherty was outside, patrolling High Street in his
Medford police sergeant's uniform. Luckily he had been able
to arrange being the walking man tonight to cover for us. A
couple of hours earlier we'd had a close call when some people in Brigham's ice cream parlor next door decided to do inventory at three o'clock on a Sunday morning.

"Tommy, what's up?"

"Let's move," his voice crackled, "it's getting light out here.
We can come back tonight."

"The hell we will," Bucky muttered.

I looked at Joe. Even though it was Sunday, we had agreed
it would be dangerous to stay inside the bank during the day.
We had burrowed our way into the space above the vault from
the optician's shop next door, and if the owner decided to pay
a little weekend visit to his establishment, we were sunk.
Besides, we had our alibis to maintain.

"OK," Joe said, "let's go."

We gathered up the tools and passed them up to Brother.
In addition to the sixty grand there were also two thousand-
dollar bags of quarters Charley found in the other safe and
whatever money Bangs had taken from the boxes. Bucky and
Charley kept swearing under their breath. The air was thick
with dust and the smell of explosives. We made our way
through the optician's shop and out the common cellar door.
The cars were in the parking lot behind the bank. We loaded
the tools into Doherty's Plymouth and Bucky's Pinto. We

covered the tools with the empty duffel bags. They should have been full. It didn't look like we were coming back.

Tommy reported back to the police department and knocked off early, saying he had a migraine. We picked up a third car at Tommy's house and then we all drove up Route 93 to Tewksbury, the northern Massachusetts town where Joe Bangs lived. I went with Tommy in his car and on the way he asked me about the goings-on inside the bank. He wasn't too happy when I told him. On his last police detail at the bank he had seen bags and bags of money waiting to go into the vault. How could there be only sixty thousand bucks in there?

We arrived at Bangs's house to the sounds of birds chirping. The sun was just beginning to slant through summer leaves, lighting the empty roads. American flags, in celebration of Memorial Day, hung outside a few of the houses on the quiet street.

We went down the cellar to divide the money. Joe emptied his pockets and started counting.

"So," I said, "we going back tonight?"

"What the fuck for?" Bucky said.

"We could do the deposit boxes."

He raised his eyes to heaven.

"You think there's going to be anything there? No way, no way I'm going back. You guys can do what you want but I ain't taking the risk."

Tommy looked at Charley. He had always stuck with Bucky and he wasn't changing now. Brother scratched his mustache and shrugged.

"Whaddaya think, Jerry?"

As I was about to answer I looked at Joe. I could see something in his eyes, something that hadn't been there before.

"Wait a minute," he said excitedly, "wait a minute."

"What?"

Joe counted out the last few bills and smiled.

"There's over a hundred grand here."

Bucky's eyes lit up.

"How much?"

"A hundred thousand dollars. I popped open a couple of safety deposit boxes, and look how much there is."

"How many boxes in there?" Bucky asked Tommy.

"Eight, nine hundred."

We all looked at each other.

"That settles it," Bucky said. "We're going back"

We divided the rest of the money and went our separate ways, agreeing to meet at Tommy's that night. I spent all day Sunday working on my boat, my stomach turning, my nerves on edge, my mind a welter of questions: What if the optician came in? What if the bank manager decided to run a holiday check on things? What if Bucky's alarm bypass malfunctioned and the cops, the straight cops, found out? We had done all the real work last night, but if we couldn't get in tonight, the whole operation would be fruitless.

When we met at Tommy's that night he told us that he had checked at the police station to see if the break-in had been discovered. All clear. Just as I did the first night, I picked the lock on the optician's shop and let everyone in through the cellar door. We moved the tools in and started working. By two in the morning four of us were knocking the hinges off the boxes while a fifth stayed above, keeping radio contact with Tommy, who was again patrolling the street.

The work was hard. The vault was hot and it was tough to breathe. Brother emptied a candy jar, filled it with water, and passed it down. He ate the candy and scattered the wrappers on the floor of the optician's loft. Dust swirled around the droplight. Busting the hinges and prying open the doors took time, and soon we were all soaked in sweat. But we didn't care—the money and valuables were piling up. We dumped cash into one duffel bag and jewelry into another. Everything else, including checks and negotiable bonds worth a fortune in themselves, we scattered on the floor before returning each box to its slot. Soon we were ankle-deep in debris. It was getting tough to move.

But the last thing we were worried about was moving. What was happening before our eyes was the kind of thing you don't even dare to dream. Lined with row upon row of deposit boxes, the vault was a library of miniature safes, with each little safe containing something valuable and surprising. This was where people kept their most prized possessions; this was where the real wealth of the city lay, and we hadn't even realized it. We found diamonds so big they would have made a king gasp. We found jewels I never knew existed—black pearls and pink diamonds and uncut emeralds. We found elaborately wrought broaches and pins and earrings that would never be worn—they were too valuable and too bizarre. There was a huge gold bumblebee studded with diamonds and rubies. There were large, bejeweled rings that I couldn't have bought with ten years' salary. And there was cash, thick bundles of cold, hard, untraceable cash. All I could hear in the vault were the sounds of hammers and chisels doing their work and the repeated words of wonderment as each new treasure was revealed. None of us could believe this. Bucky and Kenny, who handled jewels professionally, were going crazy.

"This is unbelievable. *Unbelievable!*"

"Hey," Brother said, "look at this."

He held up a sandwich he had found in a box.

"Look, there's even salt and pepper shakers. This guy was really out to lunch!"

He started clowning around, making like he was going to eat the sandwich. Charley was hooting and hollering and throwing silver dollars into the air. We were all laughing, high on all the money and jewels surrounding us.

As daybreak approached we pushed the full bags up to Bangs and loaded everything into the Plymouth and Pinto. We had broken into less than half the boxes, but we still had another night of this Memorial Day weekend before the bank employees returned. Again we drove up 93, but this time we were feeling better. Even if we didn't get back to the bank the following night, we had still made a fortune. We drove nice and easy, not attracting any attention to ourselves, and returned to Bangs's house.

In the cellar we emptied the cash onto the floor. I couldn't believe it. The stack was three feet high and five feet in diameter. I felt as if I'd just won the jackpot on "Sale of the Century." I had never seen so much money in my life. We were mesmerized, and for a few minutes we only stared. And this wasn't all—there were also three duffel bags crammed with jewelry and another five hundred boxes back at the bank just waiting for us to return!

We sat in a circle around the pile and started counting. Joe brought in cold drinks. My shirt was sticking to my back and my hands were shaking with excitement. I was so tired, so exhausted from all the work I'd done in the last two nights, that the whole scene seemed unreal. A dream. But here it was—hundreds and hundreds of thousands of dollars just sitting there. This was the big haul, bigger than any of us had ever dreamed. Figures floated in my head. I would never have to work again. I would be my own boss. I was in clover.

We all counted silently, working through the morning. We stacked the bills in bundles of a thousand. Joe kept a running total while Bucky and Charley examined the jewelry. Charley whistled in amazement as he let pink diamonds run through his fingers.

"These babies alone," he said, "are worth millions."

Bucky spread the glittering jewelry across the cellar floor and scratched figures on a pad of paper. Charley picked up a gold Movado watch.

"Anybody mind if I take this? For my wife?"

We shrugged. Sure. There was so much here that a valuable watch like that seemed like nothing. Little did we know that the watch would come back to haunt him.

As people read the paper and ate breakfast and went to the beach, we worked long and hard, counting our haul. When we were finally done I stood up, stretching my back and shaking dollar signs from my eyes.

"So what we got here?"

"Close to a million in cash," Bangs said.

I whistled.

"The cash ain't nothing," Bucky said without looking up from his pad. "Here's the real haul."

He finished adding and looked across at the field of diamonds and gold.

"What's it worth?" I asked.

He swept a meaty hand over the duffel bags.

"These pink diamonds—I'd say two million. They're very rare and very valuable. The other diamonds and pearls—at least three to four million. I've never seen so many big ones in one place."

We listened breathlessly.

"See these rings here? We pop the diamonds out of these and melt the gold down and we've got another million. Then there's the rest—you figure altogether, including the cash, we've got eight to ten million here."

"*What*?"

"That's right. And this is only the half of it. You figure tomorrow night we get the same—no reason why we shouldn't with over five hundred boxes to go—and cash, jewelry, altogether we have twenty, maybe twenty-five million dollars."

The words rang in the air. Twenty-five million dollars. Over four million for each of us.

"That," Tommy said, "would make this the biggest bank robbery of all time."

"That's right," Bucky said, "that's right. The Depositors Trust job."

I looked at my pile of dough, which would be doubled by the end of the weekend. We had each made more in one night than most people make in a lifetime. We had done it. The cops had become the robbers.

1

The Tarnished Badge

How do cops end up participating in the largest bank robbery in American history? What happens beneath that blue uniform that turns the impulse for public service into the impulse for personal gain, without any regard for the law and authority that the uniform represents? Is a police officer patrolling the streets of small-town America one day, sticking to his principles and protecting the people, when all of a sudden the thought pops into his head: "Gee, that bank there must have one hell of a bundle inside—why don't I just go in after it?"

Hardly. The process that led to that fateful 1980 Memorial Day weekend at the Depositors Trust in Medford, Massachusetts, was a long and involved one, touching many lives and reaching deep into the system. No one can understand that event without understanding the whole complex network of contacts and favors and privileges that characterizes Massachusetts business, government and law enforcement, a network that all too easily gets tangled into knots of corruption. And believe me, corruption is something I know about.

Few people like to talk about police going bad. Few people like to admit that corruption exists. But it does. And I'm not talking about isolated incidents or occasional lapses. I'm talking about wholesale, deep-seated, extensive corruption, the kind that wraps a young man in its grasp and caresses him into believing that if he wants to get on in the world there just isn't any other way to go. I'm talking about the kind of corruption that fools a public servant into thinking he is not responsible to any authority, the kind that takes three cops like Jerry Clemente and Tommy Doherty and Joe Bangs, each completely different from the other, and makes them accomplices by appealing to the single, overriding characteristic they share—greed.

Everyone has his own story. In my own case you have to go back thirty years, and even then you haven't gotten to the beginning. When I got out of the army in 1955, I was young, idealistic and eager to do well. I came from a close, hard-working family from Medford. My immigrant father had worked his way up in the world the hard way, pursuing the American dream by working night and day and saving every penny he could. He did all right, too. By the mid-fifties he had established a successful rug business, a bowling alley and a web of political and business contacts that included influential local and state politicians. There was one man in particular, a good state representative who cared about people in his district and had some power in the State House, who made sure things never got too rough for my dad. This guy, who you would never dream of calling corrupt, didn't hesitate to use his position to grant people favors. After all, the spoils system in all its manifestations is the common currency of Massachusetts political barter.

My dad knew this rep well and did a lot for him, providing all his family with rugs and giving them first-rate service. In exchange, the guy would do favors for my dad and his friends. If business was slow during the summer, he would give my dad a job on a summer work gang. He could get my dad rug contracts for government buildings. My dad was honest, but I often heard him talk about other arrangements this man had made—putting someone on the state payroll, for example, even though he wasn't working; getting someone disability pay even though he wasn't hurt. But everyone accepted these arrangements as natural methods of doing business. They were part of a representative's political responsibility. They were part of the system.

For the first four years following my discharge from the service, I worked a variety of jobs, including a stint with my dad's company. I used the GI Bill to finance a course in lock-smithing—a subject that became an obsession with me and turned out to be very valuable to my criminal exploits in later years. Then, in 1959, I reached the first big turning point in my professional life—I took a civil service exam for entry in-to the Medford Police Department. I did well (I've always done well on exams), and I was accepted onto the force. On May 17, 1959, I reported for my first night of work, clean-shaven and innocent. I was excited because I was finally in a job where I could work hard and get on. I had faith in my own ability—and in the system.

My faith in the system was compromised immediately.

I arrived at the station punctually, my uniform neatly pressed, my shoes spit-and-polish shiny, my badge, gun and club fresh in my possession. I had butterflies in my stomach. I was eager to make a good impression and gain acceptance from the veterans on the force. I'd heard that camaraderie was important in Medford, that the cops didn't like loners.

I was introduced to a few guys. The cops were aloof but friendly. I started to settle down. The sergeant assigned me to a cruiser and got me together with my first partner, Jackie Mullins, known on the force as Crusher. Crusher was a big, genial Irishman with a thick mustache and a wide smile. He talked to me with real warmth and treated me paternally. He'd show me the ropes, he said. He'd take care of me. I began to feel comfortable.

He took me out to the cruiser, telling me what to expect, educating me on procedure. The night was clear and warm and full of promise. I was a cop. I was learning my trade. But before the night was through I was to learn a lot more than I had bargained for.

About two in the morning we were cruising along Medford Avenue, looking crosswise down empty, moonlit streets and listening to the occasional crackle of the scanner. Crusher pointed out spots where he had broken up a fight or collared a burglar, but nothing much seemed to be happening that night.

"Action is the exception, kid, not the rule. Better get used to nights like this."

But just as he finished speaking we spotted a shadowy figure sprinting across the avenue and down an adjoining street, carrying what looked like a large lawn chair in his arms. Crusher flipped on the flashers and hit the accelerator. We turned the corner and eased up beside the guy. I tensed, my hand near the butt of the revolver I had not even fired in practice yet. My first piece of action.

But when I looked at the guy I saw that he was another Medford cop, in full uniform. I relaxed, a bit disappointed. Crusher and I got out of the car.

"Hey Jack," the guy said.

"Dick, how ya doin'?"

Dick leaned the chair against the idling cruiser and pointed vaguely up the street.

"Good, Jack, good. Just caught a couple guys breaking into Zayres."

He gestured at the lawn chair.

"Dropped this and took off before I could get a good look at them."

Crusher nodded, stroking his mustache. Overeager rookie that I was, I decided to get my two cents in.

"Well, let's bring the chair back."

Dick and Crusher shot each other knowing glances. Crusher picked up the chair and handed it to Dick.

"Get back in the car, kid," he growled at me.

Confused, I looked back and forth between them. He wasn't kidding. I returned to the front seat while Crusher and Dick spoke quietly. Dick left with the chair and Jackie wheeled the cruiser around, heading us in the opposite direction. After a silent couple of blocks, he spoke:

"Lesson number one, Jerry: you see another cop with a

chair, a television, whatever, you keep your mouth shut. You say your hellos and you move on your way. Whatever he's doing is his business."

He paused and held up two fingers.

"Lesson number two: don't play high and mighty. You want to be part of the club, you act like people in the club. You don't want to, hey, that's up to you—but don't expect people to trust you."

He kept talking. As I listened I learned the real meaning of camaraderie in Medford. There would be no acceptance without compliance. Stealing made you one of the guys, part of the club. If you didn't participate, you weren't trusted; it was as simple as that. The others had to have something on you so that they knew you wouldn't talk if you saw them transgress. And everybody, or almost everybody, transgressed. If you were dispatched to the scene of a break-in, you lifted a couple of items and stored them in the trunk of your cruiser while waiting for the owner to show up. And it was easy enough to justify: the crooks got away, the owner got his insurance money, and the cop got a new radio or wrench set or garden hose. Everybody was happy. I may have been shocked to discover this activity, but for a young man used to seeing favors traded in business and politics, it was an easy step to take.

But I soon discovered that the corruption cut a lot deeper. If a cop wanted something badly he wouldn't necessarily wait for a break-in—he often became a burglar himself. Night shift then became a boon instead of a pain. At any given time, two-thirds of the force was on one of the two night shifts—the four to twelve or twelve to eight—and because the shifts rotated, anyone on the force was liable to become a thief. No business was safe. A major shipping company in town was a favorite target. Cops would enter from underneath the building, removing floorboards and lowering typewriters, furniture, even refrigerators through the hole and into a waiting truck. Alarms were no problem; the cops had the experience, plenty of time to investigate and no fear of the law. They *were* the law. A department store might be completely bugged except for the skylight, so down the skylight the cops would go and out came clothes, household goods, appliances. Around Christmastime a big toy store became the center of attention. One of the cops would bypass the alarm by breaking into an adjoining laundromat, shinnying along a crawlspace above the store, dropping into the building on the other side and letting his cronies in the back door. Pool tables, bikes, toys—anything these young cops needed for their kids over the holiday season disappeared. And only the really stupid got caught because you had to be stupid not to get away with something so easy.

The longer I was in Medford, the more I realized how extensive police corruption was. It had been around a long time before I arrived, and it was not confined to my hometown. I soon learned that every Boston-area town—from working-class communities like Chelsea and Revere and Somerville to wealthy suburban towns like Belmont and Newton and Brookline—had its share. Once, when I was investigating a break-in at an electronics firm in Wellington Circle in Medford, a cop from Cambridge, which is two towns over, arrived and asked if he could take a television. He had heard about the burglary over his scanner and rushed over for a piece of the action! Wellington Circle plaza had so many stores grouped together and was so prone to police thievery that it was known among cops as "Treasure Island." Whatever you wanted was there. And again, the step was an easy one—after all, you were just picking up something for your wife or kids. And weren't you doing enough for the community? Didn't you put your life on the line?

One of the biggest ironies of police corruption is that cops do serve the community, they do put their lives on the line. Even as I was receiving lessons in nocturnal pilferage I was conscientious in other respects. One night in 1960 I was doing duty in my cruiser when news of a holdup of a liquor store in West Medford came over my radio. I had just returned to the force after a five-day suspension for "incorrigibility" during a training session at the state police academy in Framingham. Let's just say there was a personality conflict arising from me being the individual I've always insisted on being. At any rate, the only reason I was in a cruiser at all was because the captain who was officer-in-charge that night liked me and didn't want me to have to walk straight nights, my "sentence."

As soon as I heard the holdup news I picked up the route man and roared up Boston Avenue. Suddenly the holdup car went screeching by in the opposite direction. I spun a U-turn and sped after it. Next thing we knew, the two of us were staring down both barrels of a shotgun the thieves stuck out the rear window of the vehicle. We drew our guns and started blasting away, and when the smoke cleared three Somerville hoods were in our custody, one with a gaping head wound, and the chamber of my .38 was empty. It was the first time I had fired my gun in action. I was one of only three men that year to receive a medal of valor from the city of Medford. I received seven straight days off and a fifty-dollar-a-year bonus for as long as I stayed on the force. And the "incorrigibility" was forgotten. I had, as the captain later said to me, "shot my way out of the shit."

So in those early years, at least, I didn't really see corruption for what it was. It was part of a system that everyone accepted, and the very men who sincerely praised and rewarded me for my bravery and community spirit turned a blind eye to petty thievery. That was just the way it was. And it was only years later that I saw just how complete that corruption had actually become, how it perpetuated itself and turned into a kind of cancer that spread throughout a cop until there wasn't anything else inside him. And the person who made me see this most clearly was Tommy Doherty.

By the time Tommy joined the Medford Police Department in 1966, I had moved on to the Metropolitan Police. I never actually worked with Tommy on the force. After the Depositors Trust robbery, Boston magazines and newspapers frequently called us childhood buddies, but Tommy is ten years younger than I, and I didn't get to know him until I was well into my thirties.

Tommy grew up even more familiar with the network of favors and privileges than I, and he certainly needed a few of them in his career. He always seemed to have plenty of friends and relatives in high places who could get him out of the many jams his lack of conscience got him into over the years. He came from a long line of cops: his great-grandfather had been a policeman in Ireland, his grandfather a Massachusetts state trooper, and his father a Medford detective who had died in the line of duty. Tommy originally followed in his grandfather's footsteps and joined the state police in the early sixties, but he ran afoul of the hierarchy rather quickly when he was found with a stolen car in his possession. Unofficially, he was thrown off the force. Officially, someone Tommy knew cut a deal whereby a Medford officer got transferred to the Metropolitan Police (a move the cop wanted) and Tommy got transferred into the new vacancy in his hometown. It wasn't the last time he needed the machinery of privilege to get himself out of a fix.

Tommy was a cocky, streetwise kid. But he was also soft-spoken and straight. He never showed off. He had all the tools to be a good cop. Smart, careful and meticulous, he kept his cool in a crisis. He was a good organizer and he got on well with everybody. He was a hard worker who was always hustling to make a buck—buying property, fixing it up, renting out equipment he had invested in, tinkering with old cars. He wore old clothes and drove a truck. People in his neighborhood liked him.

But Tommy used his skills in both directions, fitting right into the night world of the Medford police. Sometimes he went too far and got burned. In 1972 his brother-in-law, Jackie Gillen, allegedly broke into a Woolworth's and got nabbed by a Metropolitan cop soon afterwards with an illegal gun in his possession. Tommy tried to talk the parkway patrolman out of pressing charges, saying that the gun was his. But Tommy had some enemies on that force, and the patrolman reported him to the Medford city manager. He got canned and returned a year later only by the grace of his unknown connections, who again pulled strings to get him back on the force.

I became friendly with Tommy in the seventies, when I was on night-watch and he was a sergeant in Medford. We would often meet in the Golden Egg or Howard Johnson's for coffee, then ride around in Tommy's cruiser shooting the breeze. Gradually I found out that if I needed anything—a car battery, an electric drill, even a washing machine—Tommy would get it for me, or for anyone he was friendly with for that matter. No money down, no monthly payments. It was yours. And there was no doubt about the source of the merchandise either. As one of Tommy's colleagues once told me: "Tommy is the type of guy who would steal an airplane in midair even though he didn't have a runway to land it on."

Of course, if Tommy did you a favor he would expect one in return. He skillfully manipulated the favors due him so that he could do what he liked and get what he wanted. He also used his power on the force to his own advantage. As a sergeant, and later as lieutenant, he was often officer-in-charge at the Medford station. He would send cops out on bum calls and then do his business where he knew they wouldn't appear. As I said, he was smart and careful.

One cold winter night in the mid-seventies Tommy and I were cruising slowly around Medford with the heater blasting. As snow melted against the windshield I talked about a car I was thinking of buying, seeking Tommy's advice. Tommy asked me a bunch of questions as we pulled into Medford Square. An illegally parked car attracted his attention, but it was so cold out he didn't even bother getting out to ticket it. We turned the corner and drove down High Street. Tommy pointed at the Depositors Trust Company with a gloved thumb.

"That's my bank," he said.

"What?"

"That's my bank. Some day I'm going to hit it and I'll be the richest son of a bitch in Massachusetts."

"Yeah, right. Tell me about it."

I figured Tommy was talking through his hat. With its dull, whitewashed exterior and low-key lettering, the bank seemed like the last one in Medford he should be interested in. There couldn't have been that much money in there.

"Laugh if you want, Jerry. I'm telling you, there's a lot of dough in that institution."

I looked at him. He was serious.

"You been in there?" I asked.

He nodded.

"Sure. Got my own deposit box in there in '66. In the vault at the back. Every time I go in there I see these two fat safes just waiting to be rifled."

"Who'd keep their money there? Look at it."

"Are you kidding? Anybody who's anybody's got dough in there."

He mentioned a couple of prominent local businessmen.

"You know those guys? Loaded with krugerrands they are, loaded. They got a ton of money in there. And then there's the money that isn't legit—Howie Winters, the Mob—you can bet your badge they do some laundry in there."

He whistled.

"One hell of a load...one hell of a load."

"But the place must be bugged to the gills. And the walls, the vault walls—two feet thick, right?"

"Hey Jerry, I'm not saying it'd be easy. I'm just saying that if you could do just one hit in your life, one dream score, that'd be the one to do. You'd never have to do another job again..."

His voice trailed away. I watched the snow swirling in the

headlights and thought about the long, cold night ahead. He had a point; he certainly had a point.

Tommy could say things like this to me because he trusted me. And I trusted him. I knew I could tell him anything without it going beyond the two of us. I knew he would keep his cool in an emergency and never rat on a pal. When that dream score, no more real back then than the melting snowflakes on the window, finally did become a reality, I still counted on Tommy. Even when things started going crazy. What I didn't count on was the cocaine and the jealousy and the paranoia—and Joe Bangs.

As the Medford Irish might say, Joe was a different kettle of fish altogether, a complete contrast to the cool, trustworthy Tommy Doherty. Joe was a big spender, a heavy drinker and a keen gambler. He wore fancy clothes and flashy jewelry and always had a good-looking woman on his arm. He drove Jaguars and Mercedes and owned a home in Tewksbury worth half a million dollars. Joe loved to show off his wealth—he would never allow a friend to pick up the tab and he always carried a thick wad of bills. He was into conspicuous consumption.

But as soon as he had bought you dinner Joe would steal your wallet. I had to learn this about him the hard way; by the time I discovered that Joe would turn on his closest friend or nearest relative the damage had been done. Maybe it was drugs, maybe it was greed, but Joe went off the deep end after the heist. When he talked about killing a relative or associate of his, you could tell he wasn't kidding. He had it in him.

Joe had always been impulsive and hot-tempered, however, and he made enemies as fast as he picked a fight. Unlike Tommy he could not keep his cool in a crisis. He also lacked Tommy's caution and patience. In fact, the only characteristic these two cops shared was a willingness to bypass legal methods of making a buck—and Joe was always looking for quick routes to wealth, legal or otherwise.

I first met him in the sixties, when he was running an

aluminum siding and gutter business in Cambridge. I could see he was ambitious. Even back then he was always asking leading questions about the police, looking for angles and contacts. Joe was the last man I could see in a cop's uniform, but I knew that he was aiming for a badge. I knew that if he ever did get behind a badge he would milk his position for all he was worth.

He got his wish in the early seventies when he got onto the Capitol Police, the force that patrols and protects Boston's government buildings. I didn't see Joe too often in those days, but from what I heard he started lining his pockets immediately, beginning with the state office buildings. He robbed them blind, lifting office supplies, chairs, typewriters—anything he could get his hands on and sell on the outside. Joe was anything but discreet, and he got a shady reputation quickly, both on and off the job. He always had plenty of spare cash to spend on gambling and cars and women, and he went out of his way to be noticed. He wanted to be known as a big spender.

Joe treated most people poorly. He turned on his pals and slapped women around to prove his manliness. Because he was so prone to fights, he hung around with a big ex-con named Francis X. O'Leary, nicknamed "Brother" because of his placid, almost religious face. But Brother was anything but religious. His specialty was breaking heads. He was good with his hands and even better with a baseball bat, and at six-two and two hundred pounds he was just the kind of guy Joe needed to cover his ass in a brawl.

I got to know Brother pretty well when he joined us for the heist. He was a funny guy, constantly joking, who never got upset and always kept his cool. He dressed well and sported a neatly trimmed fu manchu mustache. He chainsmoked, but back then I never knew him to use drugs. He was always looking for a score. He would pick up women and steal their pocketbooks, or give a guy a ride, sucker-punch him and steal his wallet. Most hoods in town knew Brother.

Later, when everything unraveled and Brother and I spent

some time together in the can, he told me a story about Bangs that opened my eyes to my so-called friend's true nature.

Joe and Brother grew up together in Cambridge and became partners in crime a long time ago. Brother helped Joe rob the state office buildings and knew where he could get rid of hot property. One night the two of them broke into a lamp store on the McGrath Highway in Cambridge, stole some lamps and rifled the till. A security guard saw them exiting the store via a broken window and jotted down the license-plate number of Joe's car before calling the Cambridge police. Joe was on the Capitol Police at the time. When they were picked up, Brother took the rap, saying that he had borrowed Joe's car and done the job on his own. Even though the police knew that Joe was involved, there was nothing they could do in the face of Brother's testimony.

Brother got sent up the river for five years. In exchange for Brother's actions, Joe agreed to pay his friend's wife a hundred dollars a week for as long as he was in jail. She didn't see a nickel. In the three years Brother ended up serving, Bangs visited him twice. It never ceased to amaze me that even after that betrayal, Brother continued to associate with his "friend." During the Depositors Trust job, all certainly seemed to be well between them. But Brother should have known better than any of us that when Bangs was threatened with going under, through no one's fault but his own, he'd make sure that everyone else went first.

But Bangs was a friendly guy who inspired trust in people, even those he'd already burned. He moved onto the Metropolitan Police in the mid-seventies, giving me a chance to know him better and observe his antics up close. I had originally joined the force in 1963 because at the time it paid more money and offered more opportunity for advancement. With civil service exams every two years, I could climb the career ladder a lot more quickly than I could in Medford, where exams were few and far between. So by the time Joe arrived I was solidly established and pretty popular on the force.

Though corruption wasn't as blatant on the Metropolitan Police as it was in Medford, it existed. Patroling parkways, expressways and beaches does not create the same kind of business opportunities that looking after a downtown area does, but I knew that not everything was kosher among Metropolitan cops. During the gas crunch of the seventies, for example, patrolmen were stealing gas from cruisers, and when a stolen car was recovered on Storrow Drive or in Franklin Park and towed into headquarters, it wasn't unusual for parts to go missing before its owner was notified.

Bangs fit right in and raised the corruption to new levels. From the beginning of our relationship our differences were obvious. While my thoughts were on career and promotion, his were on making a fast buck and having a good time. We became friends on the job but never socialized together. We moved in different worlds and our lifestyles were at opposite poles. I'm not saying I didn't bend a few rules myself, but I was a little more subtle than Joe. One time he rolled a drunk and got into hot water at headquarters—I straightened the situation out. During the big snowstorm of 1978 he and another cop backed a cruiser into the picture window of a big discount store in Boston and took off with a couple carloads of merchandise. Later that year Bangs approached me about buying a civil service exam for sergeant that he was due to take. By that time I had access to certain exams and—well, that's another story. Let's just say I helped Joe out. I was into things pretty deep by then.

But as deep as I was, Joe was deeper, getting into areas that I refused to involve myself in. One was drugs. After the heist Joe was to become one of the biggest coke dealers in New England, averaging at one point, he told me, fifteen grand a week—while he was still a police officer! Unfortunately for Joe, by then a lot of that coke was reaching his own brain, to the point where he could not distinguish between reality and fantasy, between honor and betrayal, between friends and enemies. Even when he was staggering through the quiet streets of Medford, high on freebased cocaine, bleeding profusely from shotgun wounds in his back and chest—even then Joe could not see the bizarre world he had created for what it was . . . but now I'm getting ahead of myself. All that is to come.

Joe, you see, was a cop who wanted to be a hood. He saw himself as another Howie Winters even though he had nothing like the network of hoods the famous Somerville mobster had working for him in the old Winter Hill gang. Joe liked to give the impression that he was connected to underworld figures, and before long he actually was. Not long after he joined the Metropolitan force Joe became known as the man to get in touch with if you wanted a hooker or a card game or a night on the town. He and another Metropolitan cop, now in the slammer because he wasn't careful enough with a suitcase of hashish and a sawed-off shotgun, would rent an apartment in the nearby town of Everett and run card games, skimming a percentage of each pot. Most of their patrons were cops, but the frills they provided were hardly legal—dope, hookers, cheap booze, videotaping sessions involving prostitutes, whipped cream and cherries—I never visited these parties, but I heard plenty of stories. And if Joe Bangs was running things you can bet the scene got pretty perverse.

But at work Joe and I stayed pretty tight, and when he knocked heads with the establishment I stuck by him; that was how I had been taught to operate all my life. You stick by your friends, doing them favors and receiving favors in return. That was the system and the system hadn't failed me. So when Joe passed the sergeant's exam in 1978 and ran into trouble with the superintendent of the Metropolitan Police at the time, it was only natural that I should help him out.

The super, who had never liked Joe to begin with, heard rumors about Joe's card games and started a campaign to deny him the promotion he was due. He put together a file on Joe, collecting statements from other officers who had attended Joe's social evenings. He wanted to initiate an internal investigation, deny Joe the promotion and perhaps oust him altogether.

Joe caught wind of the file and came to me. Late one quiet night in September I picked the lock on the super's door at headquarters. We found the files and made copies. We took the material to a prominent Massachusetts state senator, for whom Joe's uncle worked, and left it with him. He had his own ax to grind with the superintendent and gave him a call. When he started reading the files over the phone the super sputtered in rage.

"Where did you get those?"

"Let's just say," the senator replied, "that there are people out there who don't like you."

"This is outrageous...this is..."

"I hope you're in a position to reveal your sources, because if you're not..."

Joe Bangs got his promotion. And I...well, I earned a favor and added to my store of experiences of law enforcement and politics, Boston-style.

You can see, then, that by 1980 I had received a pretty thorough education, dating back over twenty years, in the complexities of police privilege. I had come to know some people who didn't exactly do things by the book, and I had failed to read the book myself a few times. There was no doubt that at some point I saw these dark deeds for what they were, but that darkness had arisen from a gray area of camaraderie and favor that in Massachusetts is very, very wide. When the details of the Depositors Trust heist began to come together, when the people and the possibilities started to surface, I didn't think twice about my own involvement. After all my experiences in Medford and the Metropolitan Police, after my contacts with the shady worlds of business and politics, after my friendships with Tommy Doherty and Joe Bangs—after all that, robbing a bank was nothing. Nothing at all.

2

For the Love of Money

On Halloween night, 1979, I drove to work with a splitting headache and major concerns about the shift ahead. This night was always one of the most hectic of the year, with bonfires raging in the parks, illegal firecrackers popping off all over the city, pranksters pulling all kinds of practical jokes and thousands of little kids wandering the streets, collecting goodies and running the risk of garnering tainted candy and razor-blade-spiked apples. As night-watch commander of the police force responsible for Boston's parks, beaches and parkways, I knew I was going to be at the center of this commotion, which would not help my pounding head. As goblins, witches and skeletons scampered by, I pulled into Metropolitan headquarters on Somerset Street in Boston and took a deep breath.

The night turned out to be relatively quiet, however, and by midnight the worst was over. I was relaxing in my chair with a 7-Up when I heard a knock on my door. Trick or treat, I thought.

"Can we bug you a sec?"

It was Joe Bangs, in mufti. He came in, followed by a hulking, smiling Brother. No sooner was Joe in the office than he was dancing around, jiggling his keys and hitching at the lapels of his expensive leather jacket. I knew immediately that he had some scheme brewing.

"Mind if I close this?" he asked, pointing at the door.

"Go ahead."

They sat down. Joe kept glancing over his shoulder, as if ghosts were sneaking up on him. Brother twiddled his mustache and looked around my office as if he were casing the joint for a hit.

"This a social call, Joe," I said, "or are you here on police business?"

Brother laughed.

"It's like this, Jerry. I'm, uh, shopping for some equipment. Video cameras and so on."

"No kidding. What for?"

"You really want to know?"

"No."

Joe's card games and extracurricular activities were common knowledge by then, and I really didn't want to hear the details.

"Home movies of the kids," Brother said.

"Yeah, right."

"There's this TV supply store in Medford," Joe said, "on Mystic Ave? I figured it'd be an easy place to pop, but I thought I'd run it by you first. You know Medford."

I looked at Brother. Recently he and Joe had done me a favor by stealing a rust-bitten Cadillac I was saddled with and sinking it into sixty feet of water off a Boston pier. I collected five grand in insurance and no one was the wiser. These guys knew they could trust me, but could they trust each other? If Brother had any doubts about doing another break-in with Joe, he certainly wasn't showing them now.

"What place?" I asked.

Joe mentioned the name of the firm.

"No way," I said. "It's bugged."

He smirked.

"No problem. I got an alarm man."

"You?" I asked Brother.

"Not him," Joe said, "a *real* alarm man. A pro."

Joe's proposal sounded too much like his usual pathetic attempts at acting big-time, so I didn't take him too seriously. If he wanted to think of himself as a big shot with connections, that was fine with me, but I wasn't going to waste much time with him. So, in order to get rid of him more than anything else, I said:

"I'm not really the guy to talk to, Joe. You should get in touch with Tommy Doherty. He's in the department there, he knows the Medford scene."

Joe's little plan would be right up Tommy's alley. But Joe did not know Tommy well enough to approach him with a question like this. Although they knew of each other, they weren't friends. Tommy knew some of Joe's friends, and he also knew I knew Joe. So I arranged a meeting over at Tommy's house, and Tommy listened carefully while Joe went over the whole spiel again.

"How good's this alarm man?" Tommy asked.

"The best."

"You sure?"

"Positive."

Tommy drummed the tabletop with his fingers and seemed to look right through us. I could see what was coming, what had been coming for years.

"You got an alarm man that good," Tommy said, "what are you messing around with some piss-ant video store? Why not hit something worth your while?"

"Like?"

"Like the Depositors Trust..."

The meeting shifted gears, moving onto an entirely different level. This was serious, and I wasn't sure what I had gotten myself into. Joe was nodding steadily and glancing at Brother, whose face had lit up like a pinball machine.

"Depositors Trust. You know it?" Joe said.

"*Know* it? I *own* the fucking place. That's my bank, just ask Jerry here. I know where the vault is, I know what's in it, I know how to get to it. I know where the alarm is and how it works. I'm not saying it'd be easy or I would have done it myself by now, but if you got a guy who knows he can take care of it, I can make damn sure nobody bothers him."

"Hey, I'm convinced."

"So what's this guy's name, this alarm man?"

"Barrett. Bucky Barrett. A bank pro. My uncle knows him and says he'll get us together—for a price."

"If we do the Depositors Trust with this guy then any price is worth it. There's millions in there."

So the scheme was born. It is hard to believe now, but the genesis of the job was as simple and as smooth as that. Four of the six of us who ended up doing the heist—Joe, Brother, Tommy and I—were there in Tommy's house, moving from a simple little video store job to the score of a lifetime in a couple of casual sentences. Easy. But why shouldn't it have been? With Joe Bangs's connections and Tommy Doherty's position on the Medford PD, doing this bank was going to be like stealing from the blind. Everything depended on Bucky Barrett. Would he know what he was doing? Would he cooperate? Would he involve himself with cops?

We didn't have anything to worry about. Joe was right; Bucky was a pro, a safecracker and a bank robber all his life who knew his job inside out. When Joe contacted him he had just gotten out of prison after doing some significant state and federal time in a few Massachusetts corrective institutions, ending up at a forestry camp in Plymouth. Knowing Bucky, I have to laugh now at the thought of him planting trees and clearing woods. He was the ultimate con, the city kid gone shady with connections with the Murray gang in Charlestown, the Winter Hill gang in Somerville (both of which were very well-known in the Boston area) and the famous Kingston gang in Montreal. He knew procedure, equipment and timing. He knew gold, silver and jewels. But most importantly, he knew safes and alarms. He had the knowledge and the touch. So Tommy and I waited with bated breath a week later when Joe, his uncle Red Delaney and Bucky met at the Ten Hills Cafe in Somerville and cruised by the bank to have a look at the rubber boot that housed the alarm at the back of the bank.

"Shouldn't be a problem," Joe told us afterwards, "Bucky says it's pretty standard."

"He go inside it?"

"Didn't want to risk it. Said we should all go down there together when Tommy's on duty so we can take a little time and do it right."

"He trust us?"

"I doubt Bucky trusts anybody. But this is a business proposition he doesn't want to miss, you know what I mean?"

Two nights later the five of us met in the parking lot of a Howard Johnson's restaurant in Wellington Circle that was, ironically, across the street from a Metropolitan police station. Joe introduced us to Bucky, a short, chunky guy with a round face and a friendly smile. A fringe of dark brown hair circled his balding head, and his close-set, cagey eyes said he was on the ball. At first Bucky struck me as the kind of guy you could push around—friendly, soft-spoken, reluctant to raise his voice or offer opposition. There was nothing vicious about Bucky, at least not on the surface. He spoke with a nervous tic in his voice and an accent I couldn't place. Later I found out that he liked the fast life as much as Joe Bangs did, and even if he was not inclined to violence, his associations probably brought him to a violent end.

It was obvious in that first meeting that Bucky was testing us, checking us out. And you certainly couldn't blame him; he was getting involved in a job with three cops and a cop's friend, none of whom he had met before, and he was a man who made a living avoiding guys like us. So he wasn't giving anything away. All those years I knew him and dealt with him after the robbery, I never knew where he lived. I knew where I could find him if I had to, since he owned a jewelry store in Lynn and a bar in Boston, but his private life he kept very private.

We shot the breeze for a couple of minutes and then got down to business.

"Anybody else know about this?" Bucky asked.

"Red," Joe said, referring to his uncle.

"I'll take care of Red. Anybody else?"

We all shook our heads.

"OK, let's go."

We drove to the bank, Tommy following in his cruiser. The alarm was behind the bank, beside a parking lot off Governor's Avenue that served the stores on High Street. High Street ran up from Medford Square, the busiest intersection in the town and the center of the business district. We parked a block away, walked up and examined the immediate area. Directly behind the unit of buildings housing the bank was a door that opened into a common cellar for the optician's shop next door to the bank and a Brigham's ice cream parlor next to that. A set of stairs led down to the cellar door, surrounded by an iron railing. About fifteen feet above the railing and off to the right was the alarm, encased in a rubber boot. The parking lot was dark and empty, and though there were some apartments across the street that overlooked us, no one could have seen us, even if he had looked directly down.

We dragged some milk crates over from Brigham's and piled them under the alarm. Bucky climbed up for a look. I stood at the foot of the crates, a penlight cupped in my right hand so that a thin beam of light focused on the boot while Bucky worked. Brother held the crates, Tommy stayed in the cruiser monitoring the police radio and Joe did his usual nervous dance even though the parking lot was pitch black. Bucky pried the rubber casing off the boot, revealing an absolute maze of wires in what seemed like a hundred different colors. Carefully, slowly, he sifted through them with gloved hands, examining their arrangement and fingering the nuts that held them in place. After about fifteen minutes he replaced the casing and climbed down.

"Well," Joe said, "what's the scoop?"

"Piece of cake. A fucking piece of cake. Nothing electrical in there, just telephone and alarm wires. I get a meter, some clips from the phone company, and it's just a matter of time before I isolate the right wires."

"How much time?"

"Month or so."

"That's a while," Tommy said. "Why don't we check out the alarm panel at the police station, see if we can't just bypass it there."

The five of us did exactly that the following night, but we discovered that the alarm would also be triggered in the company that installed it. We would have to go with Bucky's plan. At the next meeting he assured us that, though isolating the wires might take time, it would be a cinch.

"Then we get a six-volt battery, run the current out of the alarm wires and into the battery, and we can do whatever the hell we want."

Bucky's words were like magic. We had visions of getting rich by Christmas: trips to Bermuda in January, new cars and fat bank accounts for each of us. But we were soon brought down to earth. It turned out that to test each wire individually, rig up the equipment, do a dry run and take all the other precautions necessary to avoid getting caught, we would have to put in quite a few man-hours. Obviously we could only work at night, and to be doubly certain of steering clear of trouble we decided to work only on nights when Tommy was on duty. Nothing but perfect was good enough, Bucky said over and over. We needed to be 100-percent sure.

So for the next couple of months we met once a week or so, braving the frigid winter nights, huddling around the boot while Bucky did his meticulous work. He had to take the nuts off every single wire, attach each wire to a special metal clip and test it on a meter that told him what type of wire it was. Every single wire had to be tested. The alarm wires would have a lower voltage—Bucky's meter would tell us. When he needed specific nuts and clips that only the telephone company could provide, we all broke into New England Telephone's warehouse on Locust Street and did a little shopping. Again, Tommy's position on the police force was invaluable—we knew we wouldn't get caught.

As Bucky progressed we started thinking about doing the

heist over the weekend of Washington's Birthday, when we'd
have three days to work. In the meantime there were other
matters to attend to. I picked the lock of the Burns Optical
and Hearing Aid Center next to the bank a few times and cased
the place with Tommy. We knew we could get above the bank
vault if we broke through the back wall of the shop. Conveniently, the owner had recently built a loft exactly where
we had to work and installed heavy-duty electrical outlets right
where we needed them. He had installed them for a lens-
tempering unit and a lens-edging machine (similar in their electrical requirements to a drill), but he was later to get a lot of
flak from the community and from the FBI for what looked
like a fortuitous bit of remodeling.

Joe wanted a diagram of the inside of the vault, so Tommy
and I visited the bank. I stayed in the customer service area
while Tommy attended to his safety deposit box. He mentally paced off the dimensions and noted the positions of the
boxes and safes. When he came out he told me that there was
so much money in there that they had bags of it lying on the
floor. We told Bucky and he simply smiled. He knew what
this meant. It soon became obvious that Bucky was even
smarter than I thought. He rehearsed us very carefully, always
explaining every step, pointing out the dangers and pitfalls
he had suffered in the course of his career. He was putting
his experience to work for us. December passed. January. We
soon saw that Washington's Birthday was unrealistic, so we
set our sights on Memorial Day, the next long weekend. That
would give us plenty of time.

By the time Bucky isolated the alarm wires we were into
April and right on schedule. Bucky had nearly finished putting together a bypass box, a small unit the size of a cigar box
that would interrupt the current of the alarm, keep it live, but
enable us to break into the bank without the alarm going off.
Because the voltage would be maintained, the alarm would
remain intact. We were nearly set.

Mid-April we met at Joe Bangs's house. Bucky took over
the meeting, detailing duties, setting a schedule, reminding us

of the little precautions only an experienced bank burglar would know.

"OK, let's talk about equipment," he said. "First we need a drill, a good one that can't be traced. We'll need it to go through the optician's wall and then down into the vault. Anybody know a good place to get one?"

Brother said he knew a store on Western Ave.

"Good. Pay cash and use a phony company name if they ask you to fill out a card. Make sure you file off the serial number—we'll dump it afterwards, but you never know, they might find it."

"What about the vault roof?" Joe said. "It'll have metal rods running through it."

"I'm getting to that. I know a place in New York where I can get special carbide-tipped core bits that won't break, even if they hit metal. They're not what you call a common item, so you got to be careful. What we do is, drill a circle of holes and then bash through with sledgehammers—if we can. If that don't do it we'll dynamite."

"*Dynamite*?"

"Yeah. Quarter-stick should do her. I'll take care of that and the sandbags to go on top. Now, we'll also need torches, for the safes and for the metal rods."

"I got torches," Tommy said, "and I know where I can lift a couple of acetylene tanks so they can't be traced."

"Good. That'll do for the safes. I'll bring a little portable job for the rods in the vault roof."

"We gotta use dynamite?" Joe asked. He was nervous just thinking about it.

"Yeah," Brother said, "and if you're not careful it'll blow your fucking head off."

We all laughed at Joe's nervousness, but if he was like this now, how would he be when we were in the vault?

"Tools," Bucky said. "We'll need sledgehammers, crowbars, chisels, screwdrivers and small hammers."

Joe and Brother said they would provide the tools, along with duffel bags to carry the loot.

"What you do is this: wipe all the tools down with alcohol, *carefully*, and that'll remove prints. From that point on we handle everything with gloves, and I mean everything. The feds got laser technology now to lift prints and they can fucking pick up anything."

Bucky covered all the bases. He told us what clothes to wear, how to burn them afterwards, how to ensure that no dirt or debris got lodged in the crevices of our car seats and floors. He said he would supply burning rods—long pipes filled with magnesium that, when heated up, could cut through anything—which we could use for the safes if need be. He talked about how to split the dough and cover expenses. Red Delaney, who had faded off the scene after introducing Joe to Bucky, was due fifty grand for his liaison work. Certain payoffs had to be made.

"Payoffs?" I said. "To who?"

Bucky smiled.

"You think you can rob a bank just like that? You need *permission*."

"Permission? From who?"

"Who do you think, the cops? You guys are the fucking cops. You need it from the guys who call the shots in my business, that's who. For all we know the Mob's got their own money in there, and even if they don't they'll want a hundred grand or so just because—and if they don't see the dough, their style of ensuring payment ain't exactly through the courts."

We left on that happy note, agreeing to meet the following week in Woburn, a suburb west of Medford. I thought Bucky seemed a little nervous, and sure enough during the week he suggested to Bangs that we bring in a sixth man, someone who could help him on the alarm and in the vault. Joe asked him if it was absolutely necessary to get yet another guy involved; after all, a cut of a fifth is significantly more than a sixth,

especially when you make a big haul. Bucky said it was. Joe
assured us that Bucky was honorable, so we agreed. Looking
back, it is obvious to me that Bucky was covering himself.
Alarm men are usually the most expendable in a burglary gang.
They are usually the most obvious suspects, the first to be
picked up and questioned, and the first to feel the heat. Many
gangs bump off the alarm man rather than risk him spilling
his guts, and I'm sure Bucky had a similar fear, even though
he had nothing to worry about. Add to that the fact that he
was dealing with cops and you could see why he was eager
to get someone he knew in on the action. The way he looked
at it, we couldn't kill him if he had an accomplice to keep
an eye on us.

But we—or at least I—weren't interested in killing anybody.
We just wanted the money. As April came to an end we could
almost smell the riches every time we drove through Medford.
One night we all met at a Denny's restaurant in Woburn.
Bucky had the safecracker with him, a young guy of about
thirty or so who was very well-built and very shrewd-looking.
He was also extremely quiet. Bucky introduced him to us as
Charley, the name I was to know him as for over five years.
It was only after we were arrested for the crime in late 1985
that I found out his real name—Kenny Holmes.

Kenny was a relative of Bucky, a kid Bucky had helped raise,
so they were tight. Bucky had taught Kenny everything he
knew, and Kenny had learned a lot more besides. He had gone
to a school in Florida that specialized in locks and safes, and
even though he was young he knew his trade inside out. I
thought I knew a lot about locks, but I was an amateur compared to Kenny. He had not worked a legit day in his life,
but he *lived*—he liked cars and women and the high life. He
had traveled all over the world and gone through millions of
dollars. But he was also smart. With nothing in his own name,
he let his brother handle all his finances. He knew what he
was doing. And he knew when to keep his mouth shut. Kenny wouldn't tell you your pants were on fire. From the begin-

ning he was cautious and tight-lipped. He was the opposite
of Joe Bangs. I liked him and trusted him.

We ordered sandwiches and coffee. We arranged to do a
dry run on the following Tuesday, when Tommy was on duty,
to make sure that Bucky's bypass box could do what it was
supposed to. We also set up a contingency plan for the actual
robbery in case we were discovered while still in the vault.

"If the alarms go off," Tommy said, "I'll be on the outside. I'll pretend I'm responding and I'll make sure the cops
go to the front and rear doors. That way I can get everybody
out the side door, at Brigham's. I'll have my car there and
you can get in the trunk or the back seat or whatever. Jerry
and Joe could even stay on the sidewalk and stand right next
to me. Jerry's known in Medford, and the cops won't think
twice about him being there. And Joe, if you're in uniform
there's no problem."

"I'll be on duty Monday."

"Whatever."

"Another thing," Bucky said, "no paper comes out, understand?"

"Paper?"

"No documents, no bearer bonds, nothing with names on
it. They'd only make headaches for us down the road. Someone runs out of money or gets desperate, he might try to cash
one and we could get detected. So only cash, jewelry, coins
and stones, right? Cash gets split on a night-by-night basis.
The other stuff—well, we'll deal with that as we come to it.
How we doing on tools?"

Brother reported they were all set. He and Joe had brought
the drill up to Joe's house in Tewksbury and tested it on ce-
ment. It worked fine. Everything was in Brother's basement
in Somerville, treated with alcohol, ready to go. Joe had Tommy's diagrams of the vault, and I had checked out the optician's shop.

"So it looks like we're covered," Bucky said. "Dry run on
Tuesday and then we wait for the big day."

"What about alibis?" Joe said.

"I'll be working," Tommy piped in.

"Alibis are up to the individual," Bucky said. "I'm on parole right now, so as soon as this thing hits the papers I'm going to be a suspect. I'm going to arrange being out of state, Florida maybe, at some point over the weekend so I can call my parole officer long distance and have the phone bill to prove it. You guys, well, what you do is up to you."

I had already been thinking about my own alibi and I pretty much knew how I would account for my activities over the weekend. I figured the safest course I could follow would be to stick to my regular pattern of living—working when I was working, staying around the house with my wife, Mary, spending time at the boatyard and visiting a woman I had recently begun to see a lot of, a woman named Barbara Hickey.

I suppose it is easy to second-guess your past, to wonder why you made the mistakes you did after they have done their damage, but to this day I cannot figure out why I turned from my wife and got involved with Barbara Hickey. By the time our relationship was over I felt betrayed. That we ultimately became adversaries did not help matters. It is tough when someone you have been intimate with testifies against you in court. The danger signs were there from the start, but I was blind to them until it was too late.

I met Barbara in 1976 when I was a Metropolitan Police lieutenant stationed in Revere. She was a bail commissioner for the county, a job that entailed checking to see if arrested persons were eligible for bail, so she was around the station a good deal. At the time I was studying at North Shore Community College, and Barbara was doing a similar course of study at Bunker Hill Community College, so we had occasion to talk about classes and papers and so forth. Barbara also knew Tommy and Joe; her world was the cop world, and she seemed very eager to get a job in the judicial system, one that would give her better pay and better hours than being a bail commissioner.

During 1978 our relationship got closer and I started visiting her at her home. Around the time of the robbery I had developed a regular pattern—two or three times a week I would go over to her house, around suppertime if I wasn't working, after midnight if I was on the four-to-twelve shift. I'd stay a couple of hours, watch TV, have a few beers and then head home. It was easy to keep the relationship from my wife because the times I visited Barbara were times I could be working or visiting other friends. Coming up to the heist, I maintained this pattern, so that over the Memorial Day weekend I would continue, creating an alibi that was natural. To someone looking at my schedule from the outside, nothing would be suspicious. And the beauty of my alibi was that Barbara would know nothing of the robbery herself. She would be vouching for me without lying.

On Tuesday we met for the dry run. Finished building the bypass box, Bucky tested it on the alarm wires, running the wires from the boot to the cellar, where he attached them to the box and saw that the juice was flowing. After tucking the wires behind the boot in such a way that they were not visible from the outside, Bucky tripped the alarm. He, Brother, Kenny and Joe went around the corner and waited in a car on Governor's Avenue. Tommy and I, both of us in uniform, waited on the scene, listening to the radio. The alarm was silent; we would not know it had gone off at the police station and the alarm company until we heard it reported. Then it would shut off automatically a few minutes later.

Within minutes after we heard the call over the police radio, a K-9 car arrived, followed by the walking man, Arthur Burns. Tommy and I pretended we had just responded. We did a routine check and left. Tommy and I returned a few minutes later and waited to see if anyone from the alarm company would show. No one. We drove around the corner and joined the others.

"That's it," Bucky said. "That proves we can control it

with the box. Nothing to do now except wait until the end of the month. I'll go back, get the box, and see you guys on the twenty-third."

"Wait a minute," Joe said. "We still got a couple things to arrange."

"Like what?"

"Like where we gonna go with the loot?"

"Well," Tommy said, "not my house—or Jerry's. I've got a reputation around here and Jerry's associated with me. The farther away from Medford the better."

"What about my house?" Joe said. "Quiet neighborhood. Far away. And I got a big cellar."

Bucky shrugged.

"Fine. Joe's house then."

"I'm...let me tell you," Joe said, "I'm worried about down the road. I mean, they got forever to get us, right? Or five years anyway, until the statute of limitations runs out. We gonna be looking over our shoulders all that time?"

"The way we've set this up," Bucky said, "I don't see how we can get caught. Look at it this way: here's the circle."

He swiveled his finger in the air, pointing at all of us.

"Now, unless that circle is broken, if you know what I mean, nobody else can get inside."

"So we can breathe easy?"

"Hey, you never breathe easy. But if they don't get us in the first couple days, they ain't gonna get us at all. At least not unless one of us sinks the ship."

None of us was about to do that. We were ready.

3

Assault on a Vault

In early May I took my son to Florida for a two-week vacation, something we had planned for a long time. With nothing on the bank happening until Memorial Day, it was good to get away from Boston and bask in the Florida sun, biding my time. Funnily enough, I wasn't nervous. In fact, Bucky had prepped us so thoroughly that I was confident of success and eager for the day to come. I was looking forward to the job.

While in Florida I stayed with a friend of mine, a Boston cop, who owned a condo in Dania, midway between Ft. Lauderdale and Hollywood. Obviously I wasn't telling anyone about the job—a policy I followed to the bitter end, even when it became clear that everyone else was blabbing. I just figured that discretion was the safest course. By one of those bizarre coincidences that seem to litter this case, one of my friend's relatives, a well-known bank robber, was visiting him around the same time I was. One night we were sitting around the condo having drinks when the guy started reminiscing about jobs he had pulled. Subtly, I directed him to the subject of vaults and safety deposit boxes, and he told me some of his experiences. I gleaned a couple of tips—including one that we used during the robbery: when you rifle a box, the guy said, make sure you replace it in its slot, otherwise you clutter up the vault and risk injuring an ankle on the damn things. I filed that away.

Before we left, my friend paid for my son's rental car with his credit card, and I promised to drop by the McCormack

Building in Boston, where my friend was stationed, and pay him back over the weekend. Every little way I could reinforce my alibi, the better. We flew out on Wednesday, May 21, and returned to Boston. I called Tommy and met with Joe and Brother to make final arrangements for the weekend. I also called work to finalize my schedule. They had me down for the Friday midnight-to-eight shift and Saturday four to midnight. I was off Sunday and Monday and back to work Tuesday at midnight. The fit was perfect: I would be off the three nights we were to be in the vault, but I would be working enough over the weekend to create a partial alibi. By coincidence, the timing was perfect.

I hoped that Tommy's schedule would also work in our favor; having him work the nights when we were to be in the vault was essential to our plans. As it happened, Medford was having some union problems and a lot of cops were calling in with the "blue flu," forcing the brass to work overtime. As a sergeant, Tommy was due to be on duty every night we needed him.

I reported to work on Friday, then cruised over to Medford, my radio tuned to the Metropolitan channel. I was hanging out with Tommy, going over the plans for the following night when we had a chance, when the dispatcher reported an overturned peanut truck on Commercial Street in Cambridge. I was close enough to the site of the accident to respond—of course, I also wanted it on record that night that I was busy—but when I tried responding on my police radio I could not get through because the steel in the Medford police station was interfering with the frequency. I used the station phone to call in, but because my communication was over the phone the call was not recorded—at least I was later told it was not recorded, even though there was talk of a phone tape. And as my whereabouts that Friday night were later to become very important for a number of reasons, that missing tape would turn out to be crucial.

The rest of the shift was routine, and I went home Satur-

day and slept all morning. I rose about two and got my clothes
for the heist ready: sneakers, longsleeved sweatshirt, work
pants, gloves, nylon stocking for my hair and a baseball cap.
I put all these items in the trunk of my car along with my
locksmith tools. I called Tommy. Then, just as I was leaving,
the phone rang. It was Joe.

"The truck, Jerry, you know the truck?"

He was hyper already.

"Slow down, Joe."

Joe had arranged to borrow a truck from his pal of his in
exchange for a few bucks left under the seat afterwards. The
guy was not going to know where the money came from; if
he did, he'd want to know why he wasn't included in the
action.

"Bucky says no go, says the truck's too big for a quiet town
in the middle of the night. He said to ask you if you could
get a station wagon."

"No problem, Tommy's got one we can use."

"OK. So you come by Trull Street," he said, referring to
Brother's house, "right, and pick up the equipment? Bucky
and Charley'll be here."

"Isn't Bucky using his car?"

"Yeah."

"Well, just meet us at Tommy's."

"Fine."

"What are you doing tonight?" I asked.

"The four of us are going to the North End for something
to eat. It's a busy place, so there's bound to be people there
that know me. Then we'll go back to Trull Street."

"See you later."

When I got to work I deliberately took my time with the
detailing of duties. I wanted to make my presence felt. Conveniently, Tommy had asked the Metropolitan Police for back-
up for the Medford cops because of the work shortage and
because a big carnival was scheduled in Medford Square that
night, so I had more reason than ever to cruise over there.

About nine o'clock Tommy and I stopped by Mister Donut in Wellington Circle, and I was pleased to see two Metropolitan detectives, Jerry Gately and Joe Civitollo, having coffee. I made a point of saying hello and describing the Medford carnival so they could back up my alibi later. All evening Tommy had made sure he responded to as many calls as possible. With all the calls on tape at the station, the pattern could only help both of us.

By ten o'clock the carnival was in full swing, the square milling with people and kids raising hell all over the place. Tommy and I circulated, breaking up fights, restoring order and sending kids home. About eleven I slipped on a civilian jacket and walked up to the optician's shop. I checked up and down the street and then tipped the plug of the lock on the door; that is, I picked the lock but left it half-cocked so that, though the door stayed closed, it could be simply pushed open when we returned that night.

I went back to headquarters and did my paperwork before checking out and driving to Barbara Hickey's house, which I usually did on this shift. As a bail commissioner, Barbara often worked into the small hours of the morning herself, so it was not unusual for us to get together around this time. I changed at her house, leaving the gloves, hat and nylon stocking in the trunk. After hanging out there for a couple of hours, I told her I was going to drive into Boston to attend to some business, but I went straight over to Tommy's. Again, nothing was unusual—as a married man with a home to go to I was always telling Barbara I had to go see Tommy or Dick Madden, a friend of mine on the Capitol Police, so I could avoid reminding her of reality. She liked to pretend she did not know the obvious.

Bucky's Pinto, full of equipment, was already outside Tommy's house. I parked in the driveway, not particularly worried about being seen as Tommy owned virtually every house on the street. We loaded Tommy's wagon with the acetylene tanks and drove down to the bank, Tommy follow-

ing in the cruiser and monitoring headquarters on his radio.
We parked behind the bank. I went through the optician's
and opened the common cellar door so we could load all the
tools onto the loft. Bucky set up the bypass box, hooked in
the pre-existing wires and threw the switches. While Bucky,
Kenny, Brother and Joe went to work on the wall, I went outside and sat with Tommy in the cruiser. We had VHF and
police radios inside and outside the bank, the police radio to
monitor activity at the station, especially a report of the alarm
tripping, and the VHF for communication between ourselves.
Because it was possible for amateur operators to tune into our
frequency, we spoke in code, utilizing police terminology and
numbers— "one" for inside the bank and "two" for outside.

Tommy and I heard nothing from where we were sitting,
even though the others were drilling and hammering away inside. Every once in a while we could see a flicker of light in
the optical store, but otherwise there was no evidence that anything out of the ordinary was happening. Tommy listened
carefully to the radio. He had instructed the sergeant to call
him if there were any problems. Oddly enough, the only call
that came over the box when I was with Tommy was a report
of an accident outside my own house on Fulton Street, on the
other side of Medford. A drunk driver had plowed into the
wall next to my driveway. Had I been home he would have
totaled my Cadillac!

In less than half an hour Joe's voice came over the VHF
radio.

"One to two, one to two."

"Go ahead, one."

"Popcorn!"

I checked the street and went inside. There was a huge, rag-
ged hole in the optician's wall, a lot of debris scattered on
the loft floor and a cloud of dust swirling around the droplight.
As I passed into the space above the vault, I could see that
the wall was constructed with cinderblocks. The space was
huge; the building came to a peak above the vault and a false

ceiling had been put in, but there was still enough room to
stand. The entire space—about thirty feet by twelve—was surrounded by a foot-wide border that dropped like a moat between the sides of the vault and the outside wall, so it was
as if we were on top of a huge table with plenty of room to
work.

Brother hung the droplight from the ceiling while Bucky
took a cardboard template from one of the duffel bags and,
consulting Tommy's diagram, placed it on the spot Tommy
said was directly over the center of the vault. About two feet
in diameter, the template had holes puncturing the outer edge,
placed so that we would know exactly where to drill to create
a weak circle that could be smashed through. Bucky spray-
painted over the holes, took away the template and started
drilling on the indicated spots. The drill was loud, but when
we checked with Tommy he said he couldn't hear a thing.

We took turns at the drill. At one point Kenny was at the
drill. He stopped to wipe his forehead and Joe grabbed his
arm.

"Stop!"

"What?"

"Stop drilling. Listen."

We all went quiet. Voices, a man's and a woman's, were
coming from somewhere north of us. We also heard the sharp
whining of a dog.

"One to two," Joe said over the radio, "one to two."

"Go ahead two."

"We're hearing voices down here, male and female. And
a dog, sounds like it's going crazy."

"Discontinue," Tommy said. "I'll check it out. And stay
tuned to the other radio."

We monitored the police radio while Tommy stepped out
of his cruiser to investigate. He discovered the owner of
Brigham's ice cream parlor, accompanied by his wife and a
German shepherd, preparing to do inventory. Having recently purchased the store, the owner was eager to get working—

eager enough to go there at three o'clock on a Sunday morning! Though he didn't know it, his dog was whining at the high-pitched sound of the drill.

Tommy knocked at the window and asked them what they were doing. When they told him, he said that they would have to close up, that the police had been having problems in the square with kids breaking windows and didn't want any lights on attracting attention. Whether they believed him or not, they locked up and left. In the meantime we were lying on top the vault, waiting for the go-ahead. Even though the interruption lasted only half an hour or so, it seemed like an eternity.

Kenny resumed drilling and the dust began to thicken. He switched off with Brother, Bucky and me, and gradually we got all the holes done, even though the drill kept getting stuck on the reinforcement rods. We attacked the holes with sledgehammers, but they had absolutely no effect. We looked at Bucky.

"Dynamite," he said.

We took all the tools into the basement. Bucky took out the dynamite, cut off a quarter-stick with a plastic knife and brought it back up. He stuffed it into one of the drill holes, attached a blasting cap and wires and ran the wires into the cellar. We piled a couple of sandbags on top and joined Bucky in the cellar. He hooked the wires to a six-volt battery and the whole building shook.

"What the f-f-fuck," Joe said, running back and forth across the cellar. "Now we're fucking in for it!"

Brother was laughing at him.

"Look at him—he's going to piss his fucking pants!"

"You blew the motherfucking roof off," Joe hollered. "W-we'll have every f-f-fucking cop in Medford down here any minute now."

"Calm down," Bucky said.

Joe was on the edge, stuttering and shouting, looking like he was about to lose his lunch. He was so bad I started to worry myself. But I kept my eye on Bucky: he would know what to do. He pointed at the radio.

"Ask Tommy what he heard," he said to me.

I did.

"Didn't hear a damn thing," Tommy said.

"Ask him if any lights went on in any of the nearby houses, or if there were any complaints at the station."

Negative on both counts. Joe still kept acting hyper, but Kenny and Bucky ignored him. I followed them up into the loft and back to the space above the vault. There was no sign of the sandbags. Even though there was a gaping hole in the false ceiling (which investigators later thought we had deliberately made for air), the circle of holes on the floor was almost intact—slightly chipped, but none the worse for wear after a quarter-stick of TNT.

"I don't believe it," Bucky said, "I don't fucking believe it."

"What are we gonna do," Joe hollered, "what the hell are we gonna do?"

"Gotta go with a half-stick."

"Are you out of your fucking mind? A *half-stick*?"

"What do *you* want to do, Joe, jump up and down on the hole till it caves in?"

"Half a stick'll blow us all to kingdom come."

"Whaddayasay you stay up here and watch it, Joe?" Brother said.

"If a half-stick doesn't do it," Bucky said, "then we'll bag the whole thing. Any larger charge and Joe'd probably be right. Tell Tommy what we're doing."

He repeated the procedure, doubling the amount. This time the blast was so deafening and the reverberations so extensive that I thought someone had to have heard. Joe was stuttering like crazy and Brother was doubled over laughing at him. Dust streamed all the way down the building, through the optician's and into the cellar.

"I think you better check with Tommy on that one," Bucky said.

"I'm getting out of h-h-here," Joe said. "There's no way the heat ain't c-c-coming now."

We got ready to leave if necessary, but Tommy told us that, while he heard the blast, it was so muted that he doubted any of the neighbors had heard anything. No lights had gone on and nothing had come over the scanner. Because we were inside a thick-walled building shaped the way it was, the sound was deafening only inside; the building contained the noise. But that was hard to believe when you heard the blast.

We made our way upstairs through swirling dust and smoke and stuck the droplight into the space. Bingo. Even through the thick dust we could see that we were through. The hole in the false ceiling was even bigger, and again the sandbags were nowhere to be seen, but this time the explosive had done its work—all that remained of the circle were a few metal rods that Bucky quickly cut through with his portable acetylene torch. In fifteen minutes we were ready to descend into the vault.

Bucky, Kenny, Brother and Joe dropped into the vault. Our estimate was off by a couple of feet, so that instead of dropping into the center of the vault we were situated directly above a set of file cabinets. But that turned out to be perfect—the cabinets were a kind of platform that made it easy to climb down into the vault. I stayed above for the first hour or so, keeping radio contact with Tommy. Brother found it difficult breathing in the vault—with two torches going full blast in such a confined space, it was getting hot and stuffy down there—so he and I switched places. Getting through the two-foot wide hole was tough for me—I'm a pretty muscular guy—but I got in just as Bucky and Kenny were finishing work on the safes. In the meantime Joe had been doing his work on the safety deposit boxes, punching them with a screwdriver and prying at the locks with a crowbar before he discovered the convenient method of knocking the hinges off with a hammer and chisel and letting the box doors swing open on the tongue of the lock—backwards, really. Bucky was pleased with Joe's method because he had never seen it used before and he thought it would throw the authorities off his own trail.

The safes were, as Bucky put it, popcorn. Because the bank
authorities expected no one to get into the thick-walled vault
in the first place, they must not have worried too much about
the safes inside, because Bucky and Kenny opened them like
sardine cans, torching a corner of the front and peeling it down
with a crowbar. The vault was extremely hot, and at times
I thought I was going to pass out because of the lack of oxygen.

When Bucky and Kenny saw how little money was in the
safes—sixty thousand dollars—they started swearing at Tommy for misleading them and yelling at Joe to stop wasting his
time. Tommy radioed and suggested we move because daylight
was approaching. We cleared out all the tools, loaded up the
cars and drove up to Joe's house in Tewksbury. Joe told his
wife to take his mother-in-law and two kids out to breakfast,
and we settled down with cold drinks for the count. That was
when we discovered how much Joe had cleared out of just
a couple of boxes, and we decided to return.

Kenny and Bucky, who were staying in a motel and did not
want to draw attention to themselves when they returned,
showered and changed. I took my share of the cash and returned to Medford with Tommy. I picked up my car at his
house and drove home. My front wall was wrecked from last
night's accident, so I parked around the corner. I got changed,
ate some breakfast and went straight out to my boat at
Fowler's Marina in Revere. I stayed there all morning, sand-
ing the bottom of the boat and making sure the proprietor
and his wife saw plenty of me as I worked. About two in the
afternoon I drove out to Dello Russo ballfield in Revere, where
I knew Barbara's son was playing a baseball game. Barbara
and a girlfriend of hers were there, so I chatted with them
for about a half an hour before returning to the marina to
paint the boat.

Even now, over six years after the event, I can remember
my feelings on that day very clearly. On the surface I was cool
and routine. I tried very hard to appear as if everything were
normal. But inside I was nervous, excited and maybe even a

little scared. It was tough to do a job that extended over three nights, with three days in between during which I had to appear absolutely at ease. But that first day was particularly rough because we had gotten so little the first night and yet knew how much there was still left to rifle. If the optician decided to do a little inventory on Sunday, if the alarm happened to go off, if a passer-by happened to look in the optician's door—if any of these accidental things occurred, we would have to live forever with the knowledge that we were just around the corner from one of the biggest bank robberies of all time. Sunday was certainly not an easy day to get through.

I kept up my normal pattern for the rest of the day, having a beer at Barbara's at five, supper at my mother's at seven, a brief rest at home and then a return visit to Barbara's until midnight. I did my utmost at all times to appear calm, and nobody—not my wife, my mother, nor Barbara—suspected anything. It was a very odd feeling carrying on day-to-day conversation when I had this tense night-life to return to. But I did it. After I left Barbara's I drove into the McCormack Building and paid my friend the money I owed him. I shot the breeze with him for a while, and by the time I drove to Tommy's, about one-thirty or so, I was very happy with my sequence of alibis. I had seen enough people that day to make it look like I had been very busy.

Sunday night going into Monday morning was the night of the big haul, when the cash piled high in Joe Bangs's cellar and the pearls, diamonds and gold coins glittered like stars on the basement floor. Thinking back on that night is like thinking back on a dream. Exhausted, excited, amazed at the riches spread in front of me, I could not believe that all this was real. The ordinary world seemed very distant. When you are handling diamond-studded rings worth a couple of hundred grand and gold broaches covered with rubies and sapphires, it is very easy to lose your grip on the everyday. Almost any piece of jewelry I cared to pick up was worth anywhere

from a month's to ten years' salary. Bucky and Kenny, who
knew jewelry and gold, kept pointing out individual pieces
that would set any one of us up for life. The pink diamonds
that Kenny let run through his fingers for about ten minutes
were worth two million themselves. The solid gold bumblebee
covered in precious stones, unlike anything I had ever seen
before, riveted our attention. The Movado watch that Kenny
took for his wife was a work of art. As the loot piled up and
Bucky filled the air with estimates of the haul—fifteen, twenty, twenty-five million—reality drifted away in a haze of dollar
signs.

    But another fact makes that night distant for me, a fact that
got twisted around at my trial nearly six years later when Joe
Bangs did his little dance of betrayal. When we had counted
and divided the money, and Bucky had gone over the jewelry
and divided it into piles of precious stones and gold bulk, we
agreed that for the time being Joe should keep the bulk at
his house and I should take the gems. Then, with uncharac-
teristic ardor, Joe argued that Bucky should take the stones.
As a neutral party, Joe said, Bucky was the right man to hold
them. And he was honorable. I could hardly argue otherwise
with Bucky sitting there, so like a fool I handed him a gray
velvet bag worth millions. I was never to see a penny from
that bag or from the gold bulk, though Bangs was damn sure
he got his share. Besides the money, I took home only a paper
bag of pocket watches and rings, including one ring worth
seventy-five grand, but even that I gave to Bangs a week later,
when the FBI got on my tail. It is laughable now to see how
the media and the lawyers later treated me like the mastermind of the job when I saw less of the real money, the twenty-
odd million in gold and stones, than anyone else in the gang.
Kenny was tight with Bucky; Joe developed a relationship with
Bucky; Brother was a friend of Joe; and Tommy ultimately
involved himself in Joe's little cocaine dramas, all financed
by the proceeds of the robbery. Only I was left out in the cold,
and it is ironic that when the shit hit the fan the prosecution

took the word of Bangs for the extent of my involvement, especially when, by his own testimony, Bangs was stealing from the rest of us before we had even finished the job! Hearing the word *honor* from Bangs's mouth was the ultimate hypocrisy.

Before we left Bangs's house that morning, Bucky told us he had to fly to Florida that day to cover his alibi. He had informed his parole officer that he would be visiting his sister and a friend of his, so he had to phone from Florida to verify the cover. He left instructions for his remaining share of the cash and the rest of the jewels to be left with Kenny.

When I got home I was dead tired, but with over a hundred grand in my pocket I had to think clearly. For the time being I buried the cash in my back yard, covering the thick bundles in sawdust, to absorb moisture, and wrapping the whole cache in oilcloth. I buried the package beneath my above-ground swimming pool, showered, changed and returned to the marina to put my boat in the water. In the afternoon I went over to Tommy's house, where I met his friend, a tow truck owner, who took us for a ride to Malden Electric Company while he visited an employee of his who worked weekends there as a security guard. Yet more alibi material.

Bangs was on duty that night at the Metropolitan Upper Basin station in Brighton. Early in the evening he called me and said he would need a portable radio to keep in contact with the station while we spent our last night at the bank. I drove over to the station and picked the lock of the captain's office, where a radio was located. I saw a number of other patrolmen there, including my brother and an officer named Robert Narris, who reminded me not to park my car near the cruiser gas pumps. Around midnight Joe and I drove to Brother's house in Somerville, and from there we all proceeded to the bank.

That last night was nothing but hard work, opening deposit boxes, filling duffel bags and stumbling through the progressively enlarging pile of rubble and debris in the vault. By

this stage we weren't even bothering to replace the boxes in
their slots after we had rifled them. We knew now that we
were racing the clock; there was no way we were going to get
to every one of the thousand boxes, so we tried to get to as
many as we could before our six a.m. deadline. Also, there
were only three of us in the vault: Kenny, Brother and me.
Joe, still in uniform, sat in my car on Governor's Avenue and
monitored three radios: his Metropolitan radio, one for the
Medford police and our own VHF. Tommy, also on duty,
was "number two," stationed on the loft, watching us sweat
and toil below. At times I thought I was going to pass out
with exhaustion.

We passed the duffel bags up to Tommy at six o'clock, happy we were finished but frustrated at the couple hundred boxes
we had not managed to get to. We drove to Brother's house
and divided the cash. The total for the three nights was nearly $1.2 million, about $200,000 each. After expenses, my total
take was $177,000. But during the trial it was revealed that
the cash take was actually $1.5 million. The remaining three
hundred grand, according to Bangs, was skimmed off the top
by Brother and himself in two clever ruses.

The second night, at Bangs's house, Brother had taken a
couple of bundles of hundreds and tossed them into a corner
while the rest of us weren't looking. Joe picked them up after
we had left. The third night they were even more organized.
Brother carefully placed a couple of hundred grand on top
of one of the duffel bags and in a secret pocket in his coat.
When he went in the front door of his house to let us in the
cellar door he took the bag with him, put the money in a closet
and laid the bag on the cellar floor. So Bangs and Brother
ended up with almost twice as much cash as the rest of us,
which doesn't surprise me, knowing those two. They are living proof that there is no honor among thieves.

Joe went back to work, clocked out and returned to Somerville. We talked briefly about alibis and plans for the future.
Joe and Brother said they would dump the tools and remain-

ing dynamite in the Charles River. Later they told me that the bag full of dynamite, punctured so that it would fill with water and sink, floated on the surface of the river for a maddeningly long time. But when they saw it go under they saw the last possible piece of evidence against us disappear. We were a tight circle. We knew we could not be found out.

We had done it. I drove Tommy home and circled up to my house. A warm, early summer day was dawning. The birds were chirping and commuters filled the streets, returning to work after a restful weekend. But for me that weekend had been the hardest working three days of my life. I was so tired I could hardly enjoy the thoughts of money. I was a rich man now, but I counted on being richer still, by millions, when the gold and jewels were fenced. Millions. I couldn't believe it.

I added my remaining loot to the stash in the back yard. I showered and lay down, listening to the radio. As I drifted off to sleep I heard the news: Depositors Trust in Medford... professional job...devastation...no suspects as yet. Nothing to do now but rest, conserve my energy. The work was over but the action was only beginning. I was going to have to get ready to take the heat.

4

Taking the Heat

I knew from the minute I got home on Tuesday that I would be a suspect; if nothing else, my association with Tommy guaranteed it. What I did not expect was the intensity of the heat, and the variety of its sources. June 1980 turned out to be a very tough month for me. That month it seemed as if everyone wanted a piece of me—the local police, the FBI, organized crime, the media, the D.A., my own department —even though no one had anything to go on but hearsay and the unreliable guesswork of an unnamed "informant."

Not that I was unprepared. I had taken all the precautions, ranging from complete, closemouthed discretion to absolute certainty that I had nothing relating to the burglary in my house. I had told my wife and son nothing. When I was alone I dug up the money in the back yard and moved it to a safer, more distant place. I took the clothes I had worn and burned them in a garbage can in my back yard. The paper bag of watches and rings I put in my father's house next door. At work I didn't even mention the robbery, even though it was hot news and a lot of cops were wondering who had the balls to do it.

Before the gang had broken up in the early hours of Tuesday morning, we had agreed to be careful about fraternizing afterwards. We reminded ourselves of Bucky's frequent advice: lay low, don't spend any money and don't keep anything at home. The fire, he had said, would be hottest immediately after the heist. The longer we stayed free, the greater our chances of not getting burned. We had to be especially careful not to be seen with one another, unless we could do so without any suspicion being attached to us whatsoever.

It was clear that we formed three distinct groups: Tommy and I, Joe and Brother, Bucky and Kenny. Tommy and I would be suspects because of our Medford connection and Tommy's reputation. Bucky and Kenny would be suspects because of their safe and alarm background. We agreed we could not meet. Any communication between us would go through Joe and Brother who, because they were not suspects, could be seen with either of the other two groups. This arrangement was no big deal to me at the time—I didn't have any need to deal with Bucky for a while, even though he did control most of the dough—but in the long run it allowed Joe to cultivate a friendship with Bucky that he was later able to exploit. Because Bucky controlled the vast bulk of the proceeds of the robbery, Joe created a perfect position for himself: knowing that I was not going to be in contact with Bucky, he was able to assure me of Bucky's honesty, telling me to be patient and wait for my share, while he and Bucky dipped liberally into the stash, living the high life and splashing huge amounts of money from Cape Cod to Las Vegas.

But the first week after the heist was quiet, at least on the surface. Boston harbor, which had played host to the Tall Ships during the country's bicentennial, was again visited by the old-fashioned sailing ships for a week, and the Metropolitan Police had their hands full patrolling the harbor and keeping the traffic problems on the parkways and central artery to a minimum. So I had to work a lot of overtime. I did keep in close touch with Tommy, maintaining my usual routine with him and keeping my ear to the ground. Tommy had an inside track on the Medford PD investigation. In fact, he was one of the officers assigned to the bank detail Tuesday, when the manager arrived and thought someone had dropped a bomb in the vault. Tommy, who had made sure we rifled his own box when we were there, made the appropriate complaints, both as an officer of the law and a customer of the bank. According to him there was little or no suspicion in Medford, though I found that hard to believe. Late in the week I had dinner with Brother, Joe and one of Joe's girlfriends at a North End restaurant. Because of the girl's presence we couldn't talk about the heist, but I could tell from Joe's remarks that Bucky had been visited by the law. Brother was in excellent spirits, drinking heavily and eating two huge plates of jumbo shrimp.

During those first couple of days, the only reference to the heist outside our immediate group occurred on Tuesday, as soon as the news hit the street. Jimmy Tortelli, a Medford businessman with ties to organized crime, called me in the early afternoon and said he had to see me. He wouldn't say why over the phone. I knew the guy marginally—his brother was a cop at the time and I had had some business dealings with him—but the call was an odd one. We were not exactly close pals. No sooner was I in the door of his house than he accused me of pulling the job.

"No way, Jimmy, no way. You crazy or something?"

"I've heard...I have my sources."

"Yeah, like who?"

He shrugged. I knew he was bluffing.

"Well, get your sources straight. I had nothing to do with it. I only *heard* about it a couple hours ago."

Tortelli sized me up. He was a big, square-jawed guy with plenty of experience pushing people around. I could tell from the greedy look in his eye that he was mad as hell the job had taken place without his knowledge. Not to mention the fact that he was probably a suspect himself.

"You can't tell me Doherty isn't involved."

"I can't speak for Tommy," I said, "but I do know I saw him at least three times over the weekend and it sure as hell didn't look like he'd been busting into a bank."

We stared each other down. It occurred to me that Tommy must have said "that's my bank" to a lot of people—he had certainly said it often enough to me. But I wasn't going to give anything away, especially to a minor gangster like Tortelli.

"Doherty's at least got to *know* about it."

I shrugged.

"You know," he said, "I know people who would drop a dime on that guy without knowing a thing."

"So you know people, so what? Stop wasting my time. Tommy's always had enemies and they'll all be crawling out of the woodwork now. It doesn't mean a thing."

I left. Tortelli had wasted my time, but he had also done me a favor: he had hinted where trouble might come from, so when trouble did begin Tommy and I would have a better idea of how to deal with it. If someone informed on Tommy, even on just a hunch, life would become hard for him. And for me.

But Tommy was ready. His first contact with the outside authorities came when he reported the contents of his safety deposit box to the bank manager of Depositors Trust, who had an FBI agent with him. Tommy acted very natural, describing the police difficulties with overtime and the blue flu and quizzing the agent on laser technology the feds used for lifting prints. He was still on the bank detail, so he was able to watch the immediate investigation closely. The burglary generated a lot of local interest. Crowds of Medford residents clustered around the bank entrance all week, trying to get a glimpse of the action or, in the case of those people who actually had a safety deposit box, trying to find out if their own boxes were rifled. The papers were full of sad stories and wild speculation, and the streets flowed with rumors, but Tommy ignored them. He knew his reputation, and he didn't much care what people thought of him.

Then, on Saturday, a childhood friend of his, a well-known safecracker and B&E man, came by Tommy's and told him his house was being watched by two dark-suited individuals in a Ford LTD. The car was parked on a bridge that overlooked Tommy's house on Pleasant Street in Medford, and Tommy's friend noted the license-plate number. When Tommy put the number through the police computer he ran a blank. If it was not on file then it had to be a state trooper car or, more likely, the FBI.

But Tommy played it smart. He went straight to his superior, Captain John Keating, and started acting paranoid and hyperactive. He pretended he was worried about the FBI searching his house and finding the proceeds of his occasional small-time larceny. He told Keating that he knew there were people on the force out to get him, giving the captain the impression that any suspicion surrounding him was the product of jealousy.

As Tommy probably suspected, Keating reported the meeting to the FBI, making Tommy sound like a shady cop with a lot of small things to hide but with nothing to do with the robbery. Would someone who had just participated in the biggest bank job in American history come whining to his superior like a scared cat? Not likely. But what Tommy and I didn't know was that Keating had more information for the feds than we knew about; an informant had also been calling the department and mentioning names, including Tommy's and mine. Someone also called the Metropolitan Police, but no one there warned me about the possibility of a visit from the feds or told me what I should do if the guys in the dark suits came knocking on my door. I had figured that if Tortelli or one of his pals started making trouble my department would at least stand behind me. How wrong I was.

On the morning of Thursday, June 5, I came home after working the midnight-to-eight shift and went straight to bed. Before I even had a chance to fall asleep there was a knock at my door. When I opened it there was no doubt about the profession of my visitors: their dark suits, short hair, shiny black shoes and ominously bulky ribcages marked them immediately as G-men. I had rarely had contact with FBI agents, but I knew them when I saw them.

"Yes gentlemen, can I help you?"

The one on the left flashed a badge.

"Captain Gerald Clemente?"

"That's right."

"Jerry Montanari, Federal Bureau of Investigation. My partner, Neil Cronin."

I nodded.

"I have to advise you that we are here in connection with the break-in and burglary of the Depositors Trust Company in Medford over the Memorial Day weekend. May we ask you a couple of questions?"

I had to make a quick decision. I could either refuse to talk or ask them in. Obviously they didn't have a search warrant, which meant they didn't have anything on me. I did not, I reasoned to myself, have anything to fear. My alibis were ironclad. My usual routine had not been altered in the slightest. I had had no contact with Bucky and I had done nothing to draw attention to myself during the week and a half since the heist. I had nothing to lose and perhaps something to gain. If I cooperated I might get them off my back—and I might be able to point them more firmly in the direction of my central alibi.

So I showed them in courteously. They sat down opposite my desk in the basement and opened their folders. At this point they were deferential themselves, speaking politely and listening to my replies.

"We have to tell you," Montanari said, "that you are a suspect, a suspect in the burglary."

"On what grounds?"

"We are not at liberty to say. We have our sources."

The same phrase Tortelli used. I wondered if that was a coincidence.

"Hey," I said, "I'm thinking maybe I should get an attorney here."

"That's strictly your decision," Cronin said. "We can't offer you any advice on that."

"If I'm a suspect—I mean, I had nothing to do with it."

"You're not under arrest. No arrest is anticipated. We just want to ask a couple questions."

"OK."

"What were you doing over the Memorial Day weekend?"

I proceeded to tell them, very methodically, my exact movements, from my time at the marina to dinner at my mother's
house. Montanari interrupted.

"I hope you aren't waltzing us around, Clemente."

I was aggravating them. They hadn't expected my story to
be so complete, my times and alibis so well-knit. It made them
even more suspicious. I continued, speaking slowly. The only
incident I neglected to mention was the peanut truck crash
of Friday night, a memory lapse that was going to come back
to haunt me. When it came to discussing my late evening hours
I cryptically mentioned I had spent time with a friend. As I
hoped, they pressed for more information. I wanted my main
alibi to be revealed reluctantly, as if I didn't really want them
to know about her. After all, an innocent man would be more
worried about an illicit affair coming to light than being a
suspect, and I wanted to appear an innocent man.

"Look you guys, can I say something between you and me?
Off the record?"

They glanced at each other, but Cronin said go ahead, it
was off the record.

"This friend is, well, another woman. Over the weekend
I spent 90 percent of my off-duty time there, she'll verify that.
But guys, I'm, you know, a married man."

Their faces revealed nothing, but they noted the appropriate
details. Montanari reached into his folder and pulled out some
photographs. Tommy's was on top.

"Do you know this man?"

"C'mon, you guys, it's Doherty. I just told you I saw him
every day this weekend."

"Have you ever been inside the Depositors Trust Company?"

Their voices were so deadpan they sounded bored.

"As a matter of fact I was there a month or so ago with
Tommy. He did some business and I stayed in the customer
service area."

"How about the optical shop next door?"

"Yes, I think...I think I was there to price sunglasses at some point recently. I couldn't say when exactly."

They showed me pictures of Tortelli, Tommy's brother-in-law Jackie Gillen and Bucky Barrett. I denied knowing Bucky but told the truth about the other two.

"Do you have any proficiency as a locksmith?"

"I sure do. I did a VA correspondence course in the sixties."

"You could pick a lock?"

"Sure. If it was legal to do so."

I was a little nervous, but confident in myself. I had stuck to my routine so closely that I could tell the truth without arousing suspicion. After all, the only hours we were in the bank were the hours I would have normally been sleeping or spending time with Barbara. And she would cover for me; she wouldn't remember the exact time I left each night. I was certain I was in the clear. Formally, they asked me if I had any information or knowledge concerning the burglary. Formally, I said no.

"Would you consent to a polygraph?"

"Sure."

"What about a search? Mind if we search your house?"

"For what?"

"Papers, proceeds of the crime, wiring diagrams, that kind of thing."

"Nothing like that here."

"So you won't mind us searching."

"What kind of search you guys talking about? You gonna pull the rugs up or something?"

They hemmed and hawed and handed me what they said was a standard form, vaguely worded and suspiciously long. I didn't like the look of it.

"Well, maybe, I don't know...look, my wife is here and I don't, I really wouldn't want her to be here while you're searching. It would upset her. Could you come back after eleven?"

Reluctantly they agreed, but the way they looked at each other clued me into something I couldn't believe I had missed —they were taping me. I mentally scanned what I had said so far, but I knew I was on safe ground.

As soon as they were out the door I moved some items to my father's house next door, items I had received from Tommy that were in all likelihood hot. I called Tom Keough, captain of detectives on the Metropolitan Police, and told him I was a suspect in the robbery. He told me not to come to work that night and advised me to get an attorney. Later I found out that the FBI had told him they were coming to my house, but at the time he didn't let on. Next I called an attorney friend of Barbara Hickey, a lawyer she had been trying to convince me to contact for a divorce. He told me not to consent to a search and not to take a polygraph voluntarily. If I gave them permission to give me a test, the results could be held against me. If I were forced to take it, the results could not.

"In fact," the lawyer said, "you shouldn't have let them in in the first place."

"But I don't have anything to hide."

"Doesn't matter. You'll regret it, mark my words. If these guys want to make it tough for you, they will."

As I hung up the phone there was a banging at the door. The agents had returned, barely half an hour after they had left. It was nowhere near eleven o'clock.

"OK, Clemente, are we getting a search here or not?"

Their whole tone had changed; they were pissed.

"That depends," I said, stalling for time to think.

"On what?"

"What if you find other illegal material totally unrelated to the crime?"

"Well, pornography and such, we can overlook that."

"What if, say, you found a sawed-off shotgun?"

"We couldn't, I mean, we couldn't turn our eyes from a crime."

I looked them straight in the eye.

"See you later."

"What?"

"Get a warrant. Look, if you guys had something on me in the first place, you'd have me in cuffs by now. So forget about a search and forget about a polygraph."

"You want us to get a warrant, fine, we'll get a warrant. Enough of this waltzing around. And don't worry: you'll take that polygraph."

"I don't think so."

"We'll see."

I didn't know it then, but I had made my first big mistake, an error that would take over five years to surface completely, but an error nevertheless. If I had simply closed the door in their faces and refused to talk, I would have been better off. Doing what I did angered them and made them pursue me more vigorously. Talking opened a couple of doors—just a crack, perhaps, but a crack was all these guys needed. The hot seat was going to get hotter.

I was busy all day, making phone calls and figuring out how I would deal with the heat. I talked to the attorney again, who advised me to do nothing, absolutely nothing, unless I had to. I called Joe Bangs and told him the score. We arranged to meet the next morning in Woburn. Lastly I called Tommy. He had had a similar visit.

"Who was it," I said, "Cronin and Montanari?"

"No, different guys. I can't remember their names."

"What'd you tell them?"

"Jesus, Jerry, I didn't tell them nothing. You think I want heat? I didn't let them in the fucking door. They asked me about Jackie, about Tortelli, about you. I kept it pretty vague. They wanted to see my tools, my fucking tools. I said no way. I said give me a fucking list and I'll show you what you want, but no way are you going through my things. No warrant, Jerry. They're just trying to bust my balls."

"How'd they get on us so fucking fast?"

"Somebody's dropping names at the station, so they must be doing it with the feds too. Or maybe the station told them, I don't know. I'll bet Tortelli's tied up somehow."

"Yeah, he already accused me."

"It wouldn't surprise me if he or one of his pals was doing the informing just for the hell of it. He's had it out for me for a long time, you know. But what can they do, Jerry? Like Bucky said, if they don't grab us in the first couple days then we're home free. They didn't even have a warrant. All we gotta do is sit tight, pal, sit tight."

The next day I got a call from a local news reporter who hounded me about allegations that I was a suspect in the heist. I told him I had no comment. I met Joe Bangs in the parking lot of Howard Johnson's on Montvale Avenue in Woburn. We drove up to a residential area, got out and went for a walk. I was worried that the FBI might have bugged my car. I told him about my meeting with the feds and my concern for the bag of rings and watches in my father's house. We arranged for him to come by the house later that morning and pick up the bag. Once I had gotten rid of the bag I was more comfortable. There was nothing they could pin on me now, even if they got a warrant for every house on the street.

I drove into work that afternoon and met with Captain Keough. He took notes while I went through the same spiel I had with the FBI, accounting for every hour of that weekend, but again failing to mention the peanut truck incident of the night of the twenty-third.

After Keough took my statement he referred me to the deputy superintendent, John McDonough. McDonough relieved me of duty, saying that I should stay away from work until things cleared up. There was something about his tone that I didn't like. It was as if he didn't trust me, as if I were presumed guilty until I proved my innocence. Of course I was guilty, but I was acting as if I were innocent and thinking like an innocent man. He now admitted openly that the FBI had come to him, but he acted as if he was on the side of the feds instead of backing me up. He said I could start taking the forty vacation days I had accrued over the years, even though the force was initiating the action. I didn't like the treatment. I may have been guilty of the crime under investigation, but at the time my defenses were up just as if I had done nothing. When someone does not, or should not, know you are guilty, your reaction to punishment is exactly the same as if you were innocent. That reaction is an important part of the mentality of someone who has committed a crime, a point that the ordinary citizen often does not understand.

I returned to Medford worn out. I had gotten very little sleep over the last three days, days when the tension level was at a peak. I had the FBI on my tail. I faced a job crisis. Someone was passing my name to the authorities without any evidence. So far I had weathered the storm, but the pressure was mounting. I thought about Bucky's advice and took comfort in that. I thought about the buried money and the millions coming to me. It will all be worth it, I thought, it will all be worth it.

Rather than going home I drove straight to Barbara's at five o'clock. I had to let her know about the FBI and my department; no doubt they'd be coming to her next. She looked concerned, but I told her not to worry, that there was no way they could carry this thing much further. If she simply told the truth there would be no problem.

After our talk I went into the kitchen for a beer, pleased that I had reassured her. She turned on the television and almost immediately started yelling.

"Jerry, get in here, get in here quick."

I ran back into the living room. She was pointing at the TV.

"Your house, it's your house!"

"Shit."

She was right. Some popcorn-talking excuse for an investigative reporter had yielded to the hearsay and put my own house on the six o'clock Channel 7 news. He stood there blabbing away while the camera zeroed in on my front door and nearby street sign.

"*. . . by the FBI as a suspect in last week's multi-million-dollar robbery of the Depositors Trust Company in Medford. The suspect, a captain on the Metropolitan Police force, has been temporarily relieved of duty while. . . "*

"At least they didn't say your name."

"Say my name? What fucking difference does it make? Look, there's the street sign, for Christ's sake, everybody in Medford'll know who the fuck they're talking about—oh shit, look."

Now my wife, Mary, was on the screen, rushing into the house. Fortunately she said nothing. The reporter talked as if he had made a coup. I watched with the bizarre feeling of seeing my own life suddenly blown into the distorted bubble of celebrity. I didn't like it. Someone had done some major informing, and the list of possible gabbers—the FBI, Tortelli and his pals, some jealous hood—was long. I switched off the TV and called Tommy. He had not seen the news.

"Why are they after me, Tommy, why are they trying to break my balls?"

"Hey Jerry, you're a captain. I'm a lowly fucking sergeant."

"I'd just like to know who started all this shit."

"I think it may have something to do with the rumors."

"What rumors?"

"Where you been living, pal? Didn't you hear? The Mob's supposed to have had some big bucks in the bank."

"Oh shit."

"And you can be damn sure that if they hear our names tossed around they'll want to talk to us about reimbursement."

"You think it's true?"

"How do I know? But one thing's for sure—if it is true we won't have to wait long to find out."

All I needed was to have some crazy Mafia guy threatening me and giving me a hard time. My head was starting to throb and I could feel a fist of pressure forming in my chest.

"Tommy, I just can't deal with that right now."

"You can't deal with it? You better learn to, pal."

"Too much to worry about, you know what I mean?"

Tommy just chuckled. He knew what pressure was. He knew that the whole thing was only beginning.

"Hey Jerry—my house ain't the one on TV."

He was right.

5

Flight of the Stool Pigeon

Sometimes the past can burn you. People you knew in a troubled youth or words you said in a moment of indiscretion can reappear years later like hot coals under ashes to scorch you. Yesterday's acquaintances can become today's enemies. And when your back is up against the wall, as mine was after the burglary, those enemies start to line up across from you like gunmen in a firing squad.

At first I didn't take much notice when the name Vernon "Gus" Gusmini started popping out of people's mouths during that critical June of 1980. I had known Gus a long time and it didn't surprise me that his name should appear after an event like the Depositors Trust heist. Gus was a small-time hood on the periphery of a lot of shady activity over the years, so when rumors of Mob money started flowing it was natural to hear Gus's name in their wake. He was just the kind of guy who would try to horn in on a deal after the dust had cleared, a harmless blowhard who pretended he was big time. Somebody like Tortelli could cause problems, but Gusmini? When people started saying he was the informant and he was connected to the crime, I didn't spend too much time worrying about him. But soon I was sorry I had ever heard his name; by the end of that month he had turned from a ghost of the past into a living reminder that my own situation could easily become a matter of life and death.

I had known Gus since he was an angelic little parochial school kid, liked by his classmates and doted on by the nuns. No one would have predicted a life of crime for Vernon. A classmate of my brother at Medford High, he was the kind of kid bullies instinctively picked on, the favorite of teachers with his clean collars and scrubbed, chubby hands. His schoolmates used to joke that he was most likely to run a flower shop. His parents lavished everything on him—fine clothes, the best cars, plenty of spare cash. Whatever the rest of us had to work hard for came easy to Gus. He was an only child who got used to the good life early and spent most of his time looking to make it better.

If you had known Gus as a kid you would never have dreamed he would become a con. But it was like him to go the easy route to wealth and influence. The problem was, Gus never quite measured up. He was always trying to be a hood, but he remained a solitary figure on the fringes of organized crime, someone who knew the right names to drop and the right places to frequent but who never really became the figure he imagined himself to be. Like Joe Bangs he wanted people to think of him as a big shot with ties to the major gangs and plenty of influence in the underworld, but whenever a real criminal challenged him, Gus would back down. His career was littered with botched deals and empty bravado.

Gus's first real foray into the gray area of the underworld came when he got into the nightclub business. He started off with a club on Route 1 called the Cabaret, one of the first Boston-area clubs to have strippers, but repeated confrontations with the state police forced him to sell, and he reinvested in a restaurant and motel in Chelsea called the New Market, which he eventually lost to the Somerville gangleader Howie Winters. He returned to Route 1 with the purchase of another club, Yesterday's, which was situated next to the Kowloon Restaurant in Saugus. He still owned Yesterday's at the time of the robbery. Though Gus wanted people to think his places were Mafia hot spots, they always seemed low-rent and seedy beneath their glitzy exteriors and fancy lights. They definitely reflected the personality of their owner.

Gus was always looking for an easy buck. He developed business connections in Canada through which he trafficked drugs and stolen cars. He was part owner of a club up there and regularly shuttled back and forth between Montreal and Boston. He was continually looking for cons who could help him out with his schemes, but he rarely pulled anything big-time. In the mid-seventies he joined forces with two men named Ricardo Oulette and Billy Oldham, who Gus said were the best alarm men in the country. Once Gus hinted to me that if if I knew of a bank his men could hit he would make it worth my while, but I knew better than to involve myself with him. I certainly did not, as people later claimed, show him blueprints of the Depositors Trust.

But Gus was also friendly with a lot of cops, especially in Medford. He had grown up with many of them and knew them to see. He often served cops half-price drinks at his clubs, a typical favor, and he even sold his Medford house to a police-man when he moved into a big colonial in the more prosperous Boston suburb of Stoneham. And he knew the feds. He was on three years' federal probation for passing bad checks through a bank in Marblehead, Massachusetts.

In October 1978 I had done one of those little favors that can be twisted into something completely different. A Metropolitan cop I knew named Billy Thompson busted Oulette and Oldham at a Mister Donut in Wellington Circle, where he found them with over $100,000 worth of drugs and over $4,000 in cash. Gus called me after the bust and asked if I would talk to the arresting officer and simply ask him to tell the truth regarding the arrest. Gus and his pals were under the impression that the arrest was illegal and that the cop was going to lie regarding the collar. Since I knew Billy I asked him about the bust and he told me he intended telling the truth. That satisfied me, and I relayed this apparently harmless information to Gus. I also discussed the matter with Thomas Keough, my immediate superior, who said there was nothing wrong with my procedure. Two years later, however, that favor came back in an unexpected way.

But more than favors came back. After disappearing from my life for almost two years, Gus himself popped up again on June 15, when he telephoned my house. I was not at home. Gus told my wife that he had to speak to me soon, that he was going on a fishing trip and wanted to borrow some equipment. Well, Gus was fishing all right, but he didn't need a rod and reel for what he was after: he was after my ass. He left a number.

I was with Tommy when my wife gave me the message, and we were both suspicious immediately. The timing was too coincidental. Tommy was now certain that Gus was the informant who had given our name to the Medford PD and the FBI. How right he was we did not find out until later, but by the time he called my wife, Gus had been in contact with the authorities for almost three weeks. Watch, Tommy said to me, he's going to hit you with a new angle.

Curious, a little nervous, we drove to the Big Dipper coffee shop in Somerville, where we were to meet Joe Bangs. Joe was keeping me abreast of developments in the Metropolitan Police while I did my forty days of fasting. The world, it seemed, was turning against me. My son was being taunted on the streets and my wife was getting dirty looks. The phone would ring in the middle of the night and click silent when I answered it. Kids threw rocks at my house. I had not heard from the FBI since their friendly visit, but I soon had my suspicions confirmed—that they had contacted my department, which was going to make life hot for me. So far, Barbara Hickey had been left alone, but keeping her calm was a job in itself, and I knew it was only a matter of time before the FBI gave her the grill as well. The state police had also joined the hunt, which I found out when a friend of mine appointed to the case, Trooper George McGarrity, removed himself from the case when he heard I was a suspect. When he asked me about it I denied involvement, but I did hint that I suspected who did it. So now Gus was getting in on the action. Amid all this heat it was good to have Tommy and Joe to turn to.

Only they knew the truth. Only they could give me moral support.

I called Gus from a payphone across the street from the coffee shop. When he gave me another number to call him at twenty minutes later, I knew something was up. The number turned out to be the Kowloon Restaurant next to his club in Saugus. Gus answered with a weak, wheezy voice.

"Jerry, I ain't feeling so good."

"What's up, Gus?"

"Well, I got paid a little visit a couple days ago, Jerry, a little visit having to do with the Depositors Trust job."

"So why call me?"

He coughed.

"I ain't gonna lie to you, Jerry. They think you did it."

"Wait a minute, Gus, who are we talking about?"

"We're talking about the big guys, we're talking about the men who run things around here, you know what I mean?"

"What are you saying—North End, Winter Hill, what?"

"Here is what I know, Jerry: the Mob had money in there and they want it back. Three guys came up to my club—from a big South Boston gang, I believe—and took me for a ride. They put a fucking hood over my head, Jerry, and I thought I was finished, gonzo. They drove me around for three fucking days and kept me in a motel room at night. I didn't know where the hell I was. They wanted information on the Depositors Trust. They wanted to know who and how, you know what I'm saying? I told them I couldn't give what I don't have. They had an ice pick, Jerry, a fucking ice pick, and they sliced me up pretty bad."

He coughed again. I was swearing at myself for not taping this conversation. The papers that morning had been full of Mob rumors—the Winter Hill gang had $800,000 in Depositors Trust, they said, the North End Mafia a million. One paper said that the Mob knew who the thieves were and wanted to do something about it but were worried by the presence of the FBI. Gus's story could have been legit, but knowing his background I figured he was just trying to blackmail me. Or, possibly, he was working for somebody else.

"You OK Gus?"

"I'll live. But for a while...these people don't usually release you, they *dispose* of you, you know what I mean? They had a machine gun to my head the whole time."

"I understand what you're saying, Gus, but I wasn't, I mean I wasn't involved."

"Well, whatever. But they told me to relay a message to you and Tommy Doherty. They said they had ninety-six grand in there and they want it back. And every day that goes by when they don't get their money is another ten thousand."

"Gus, stop right there. I have no idea who did it, do you understand? What makes them think I had?"

"They know everything about you, Jerry, they have a folder full of shit on you, pictures, stuff about your life. A complete profile."

At the word *profile* the conversation took on a whole new complexion. Only one organization used that term, and it wasn't the Mob. Was it possible, I asked myself, that Gus of all people was in cahoots with the FBI?

"How many times do I gotta tell you, Gus?"

"I know, Jerry, I know. I mean, I'm caught at both fucking ends, you know? I'm just relaying the message. We're talking about heavy-duty hoods here, the kind that...well, they said they'd put your hand in a meat grinder."

"*My* hand? You know what it is? They saw my fucking house on TV and now they're trying to blackball me. That TV piece was horseshit, Gus, total horseshit. Somebody somewhere mentioned my name and now I've got the whole city on my case. But if they mess with me they'll have to mess with my whole department. They know that, don't they?"

"Jerry, I don't know what they know. But listen, I gotta go. Call me tomorrow at noon. At my house, OK? I'm supposed to see them at one."

"Right."

"Talk to Doherty, just talk. Look, these guys don't care if there was sixty million in there, they just want their share."

"I'll call you."

This arrangement suited me fine. If Gusmini wanted to play hardball, then I could play too. I'd tape the conversation and really get his ass in a bind.

I talked about the conversation with Tommy and Joe. My FBI theory did not sound so far-fetched once we reviewed the evidence: even though Gusmini was on federal probation, he had traveled freely between Canada and the US; many of his former associates in crime were now in jail, even though he had managed to maintain his freedom; and his name had come up in both interviews Tommy and I had had with the feds. Without a real case to work with, the FBI could easily be using Gusmini to try to get Tommy and me to confess, or at least compromise ourselves. And if the Mob really had taken Gus for a ride, why had they let him go with a few jabs from an ice pick? I didn't doubt for a second that Gus would tell the FBI he knew who did it and then cooperate fully in exchange for a reward or immunity from another of his many crimes. But Gus, of course, had nothing to go on but his instinct, and though his instinct was right, he had no evidence. All we had to do was stand firm.

The next day Tommy and I drove up to Stoneham, to Gus's house, and called from a nearby payphone. He told me to give him ten minutes and gave me another number. Tommy and I, driving a battered old yellow GTO, slumped low in our seats and watched his front door. Gus waltzed out in a shortsleeved shirt, looking none the worse for wear after his battles with an ice pick. He got into his Caddy and drove to the Redstone Shopping Center, Tommy and I tailing him. He parked in front of one of the stores, got out and waited near a payphone. I drove down a couple of stores to another phone. Gus was in full view. I attached a portable recording device to the receiver and dialed the number. I had to goad him, to get him to make concrete accusations that would hold up in a court of law.

"Yeah."

"It's me."

"You know, Jerry, I've been thinking about this whole thing. Between you and me, I really don't care if you did or didn't...it has nothing to do with me."

"Hey Gus, I told you before—you know what I'm capable of and what I'm not capable of, and there's no way I'm doing a job like that."

"I don't understand it then. I mean, I stuck up for you. I said there was never any question of you doing jobs like that in the past, but somebody gave them your name. And mine."

"Answer me a question. Is it..."

I mentioned two underworld figures whom I remembered Gus talking about, two guys that he bragged he knew well. He paused and went for the bait.

"Yeah. Absolutely. They had me for two days, with a couple of other guys."

"Two days. Sticking you with an ice pick."

"I'm not going to lie to you, Jerry."

"How bad did you get hurt?"

"I'll tell you the truth—I thought I'd never walk again."

I could see him from where I was standing, healthy as a lifeguard.

"I'm not trying to make problems for you, Jerry, but if you can turn me to somebody that can take the heat off me temporarily so I can get my bearings here, I'd appreciate it. What am I gonna do, look over my shoulder the rest of my life? I don't want to live that way. But if, you know, they get their piece then that'll be the end of it."

"So you think they mean business?"

"They fucking mean business, yeah, and the next time they pick me up they'll want me to go for ice cream with them, you know what I mean?"

I could see Gus gesturing into the phone, hamming it up.

"Sounds like a fucking scam to me, Gus. I don't have any

fucking knowledge, it's as simple as that. I don't know either of those guys. I mean, I thought they were *your* pals."

"Associates...sometimes."

"And you're telling me they've got a whole folder on me. A *profile*. How do I know a couple wise guys didn't just read the papers and decide to play games with me?"

There was a long pause.

"Listen, Gus, I spoke to Tommy. He said no way was he involved in this."

"Jerry, Jerry...I was thrown to the wolves, and they're not going to lie to me. I had a machine gun at my head. I'm fucking scared to death!"

"I'm not doubting your word, Gus."

"I've got both angles after me now. Both ends. And the bottom line is, these guys are going to get what they want and that'll be the end of it."

"So what are you saying, they going to take me out, is that it?"

This time I waited through his pause.

"Yeah."

"And Tommy."

"Whatever it takes."

"They'll be doing it for nothing."

"These guys will go through twenty bodies to get to one, you know, that's how they operate."

"How many guys we talking here, Gus—three, four?"

"No, no...a dozen or so."

"A fucking council."

"You know, if you could talk to them, Jerry."

"What, are you nuts? They want to take me out and you're telling me to talk to them?"

"Might take some of the heat off."

"One to one, maybe, if they want to see for themselves whether I did or didn't do it, but I'm not going to walk into the fucking lion's den, that's ridiculous. None of this bullshit with the whole crew, I mean that would be fucking suicide."

"I'm just trying to...we're both in this, Jerry."

"Well I don't intend to get a fucking hood put over *my* head, Gus, especially for something I have absolutely no knowledge of."

"They said they're not kidding. They said they'll show you what they can do."

"Yeah?"

"Call me tomorrow, Jerry. Think it over. I'll stall them. If I can just give them a hint...you know, if you have something to give them..."

"I don't have anything to give."

"...then they'll go away..."

"*I don't have anything to give.*"

"All right."

The recorded operator interrupted: *"Please deposit five cents..."*

"I'll talk to you tomorrow, Jerry. Give me a call in the morning."

The phone went dead. As we watched him saunter back to his car I suggested to Tommy that we confront him right there and scare the hell out of him. I would have loved to have seen the look on his face when I waved the tape under his nose and asked to have a look at his wounds. But Tommy wisely told me to take it easy. If he was fronting for the FBI we did not want to show our hand. We had a unique opportunity here.

I didn't waste any time. As soon as I had made a duplicate of the tape I took it straight to my superiors at the Metropolitan Police. But even before I went there I decided to cover all the bases—I contacted a friend of mine who knew the Mafia kingpin Gennaro Angiulo and, under the excuse that I was privately investigating the case, had him find out from the Mob if there really was any dirty money in there. While my friend ran his errand, I went to Captain Keough and Superintendent Laurence Carpenter and played them the tape. They were speechless. I wanted to make it clear to them that I was willing to be cooperative, though I expected their support in return. For obvious reasons I was eager to keep the FBI out of the affair.

"This is a state crime," I said. "We should contact the state police."

Carpenter toyed with his pencil. At that time I didn't know that he had already been in extensive communication with the feds.

"I think," Carpenter said slowly, "that this may be a matter for the federal agents."

"That would be a very bad idea," I said.

Carpenter stiffened. He was a product of the FBI academy and his federal loyalties ran deep.

"Why?"

"I have reason to believe," I said, "that Gusmini may be working with the FBI."

"That's ridiculous," Carpenter said coldly, "the FBI is not in the business of extorting police officers."

Keough wasn't saying anything and Carpenter insisted on doing things his way. I couldn't make him budge.

"Tell me this," I said, "when am I coming back to work?"

"The situation will remain the same for the time being."

"Why? What's happening here? I made a report."

"We may need a fuller, official report from you next week. And there is the question of a polygraph. Would you be willing to take one?"

Montanari's threat came back to me, and I saw now that the FBI had been more active than I thought.

"Willing? Let's put it this way: if I'm ordered, no problem. But I know my rights and no way am I volunteering."

I left there feeling betrayed. Something was happening behind my back and I didn't like it. But I didn't have too much time to brood, because that night all hell broke loose.

First, I discovered that the Medford PD had ordered Tommy to take a polygraph. Almost immediately, Tommy, complaining of chest pains, checked himself into a Medford

hospital. I wasn't too concerned about his health. What I did
worry about was what that order implied: the FBI was starting to tighten the screws. No wonder Carpenter was being so
firm. When I called a friend on the Medford force, he dropped
another bomb on my lap. Gusmini had been in official contact with the department for the last week, during the same
period when he was supposedly being ferried around Boston
with a machine gun to his head. I asked him if he was certain, and he gave me the details.

The previous Monday, June 9, Gusmini had called Sergeant
Paul O'Riordan of Medford and asked him to meet him at
Howard Johnson's at Wellington Circle that night. O'Riordan knew Gus since childhood and occasionally received information from him in his capacity as a police officer. When
the two of them met, Gus floored O'Riordan with the statement that he could furnish all the information necessary to
collar the Depositors Trust robbers. He wanted O'Riordan
to act as his go-between with the FBI and he wanted a half
million bucks for his trouble. He said he'd cut O'Riordan in
to the tune of a hundred grand.

O'Riordan couldn't believe his ears. When he told Gus he
did not think the feds would go along with the request, Gus
said: "You go talk to them. They'll know what I'm talking
about." But O'Riordan went to Captain John Keating, the
same man who had contacted the FBI after Tommy complained, and together they notified the feds. The bureau
seemed completely unfazed by Gusmini's demands—they even
told O'Riordan he could keep the hundred grand as long as
he notified the IRS. O'Riordan met with Gus again the following night and a third time on Thursday, June 12. Basically,
the same information passed between them, with O'Riordan
relaying messages to the FBI. The whole set-up struck O'Riordan as being very strange, and when both Gus and the FBI
stopped trying to contact him after the twelfth, he thought
that they had finally gotten in touch with each other.

I was now more certain than ever that Gus and the FBI were working together. The curtailment of contact with O'Riordan coincided with Gus's first call to my wife; the FBI had exhausted one angle and started on another. I cursed Carpenter for his loyalties. If we had let the state police handle it, they may have discovered the scam and caused some embarrassment that the G-men deserved.

But I had even more to worry about. That evening my son was nearly run over by a menacing guy on a motorcycle. Then I got a phone call late at night saying that I had a lot of enemies in the Metropolitan Police and I'd better stay away from Barbara Hickey's house. Now I knew the feds had spilled the beans to my department; now I knew my department was operating behind my back instead of coming out openly with support; now I knew I wasn't necessarily safe—or my family for that matter. What I didn't know was where the danger was coming from—other cops, the FBI, Gusmini, Tortelli and his pals, the Mob, some local crackpot who had seen my house on TV—and I was worried.

The next day the Boston papers were full of stories about the robbery. The *Boston Globe* alone had three stories, including the suggestion that there was over two million in Mob money in the vault. There was also mention of two police officers involved, though no names were printed, and a story on Tommy's hospitalization after being ordered to take a lie detector test. Sources told the paper that the FBI was "pretty confident" it had a strong lead.

I spent some time on the phone. My contact with Angiulo reported back with good news: according to the Mafioso there had been no Mob money in the bank. "Tell him not to worry about it," was his message for me. With that load off my mind I called Gus. No answer. Had I seen the last of him? I didn't know, but in the meantime I had more personal matters to attend to. My wife was very worried about the possible attempt on my son's life, the Metropolitan Police were not returning my calls, and Barbara Hickey was getting paranoid.

She swore there were men watching her house. I told her I'd come up and check things out.

She was working late and I didn't get to her house until after one in the morning. Upset, highstrung, she accused me of causing problems, and it took me quite a while to calm her down. "Are the FBI going to interview me or not?" she wanted to know. I told her what I knew about the FBI. How they were working now was anybody's guess. Nothing out of the ordinary happened until four o'clock, when I saw three cops in a Metropolitan cruiser go slowly by. I ran out to my car and took off after them. After a long chase I pulled them over on the Revere Beach Parkway. The three men were all officers: Daniel Gately, Jake O'Brien and Tony LaConti. Gately was a longtime enemy who had bumped heads with me on a number of occasions. We did not like each other; he had spent a good deal of his own on-duty time watching Barbara's house, so I wasn't surprised to see him in the car. But the presence of the other two was significant. LaConti was behind the wheel. He rolled down the window as I approached.

"Hey, Tony," I said, "if you want me, knock on the fucking door."

"What are you talking about, Jerry?"

"You know what the fuck I'm talking about. Stay off my back or I'll really give you something to investigate."

"What have we done?"

"You know what you've done."

I am not a violent man. I have only ever used force on the job, and even then only when necessary. But at that moment I was sorely tempted to take the 9mm Colt pistol I had with me and blow these guys away.

"Let me tell you assholes something—I'm off duty, and as long as I am I can do what the fuck I want. And I don't need you guys trying to break my balls."

I banged the roof of the car with my fist so hard that they jumped. A captain, a lieutenant and a sergeant. That told me something—somebody was out to get me.

The next day Gus came by my home and, not surprisingly, changed his pitch. His mere presence at the house told me the feds were getting desperate. They saw I wasn't taking the bait, but they still thought I was stupid enough to go for their ridiculous scam. The men he dealt with, Gus now said, would be happy with only $25,000.

"No kidding, Gus. That's strange. Two days ago they're going to put my head on a platter, and now they're going to be happy with only twenty-five grand?"

"I did a lot of talking, Jerry, a lot of talking."

"I'm sure you did."

"The wise guys would be satisfied, and they'd make sure you weren't hassled."

I was seated at my desk. Gus stayed at the far end of the room, leading me to believe he was wired. Also, even though it was a warm summer day, he was well bundled up—obviosly he did not want me to see that the ice-pick scars had miraculously disappeared.

"What can I tell you, Gus, I'm not involved. I don't have the money."

He left quickly, but not before my wife, who was walking home from a friend's, saw the car he'd arrived in, an official-looking Ford with two passengers who averted their faces. I had no doubt now about his associates.

But my wife had other concerns. That weekend there was another apparent attempt on my son's life. People were tossing bottles at my house from passing cars and smashing windows. Even though I had changed my phone number, the harassing calls continued. Naturally my wife, who was home a lot on her own, was worried for her life as well as our son's. I was worried for both of them. So when my superiors notified me the following Tuesday that they wanted to put my family into protective custody, I accepted. The move would pacify my wife and allow me a little breathing room. The police were worried about Gusmini's threats. They could not accept what

I knew for certain, that Gus was working for the FBI, and they did not have the Mob's word, as I had, that it had no money in the bank. So they could only conclude that organized crime had it out for me. Even though I knew they were wrong, I could see the benefits of accepting their version of events and going into protective custody—it would look good, and it would create an image of an innocent, harassed officer that might balance all of the negative media attention I had been getting. So I said OK.

I thought that this move would end my contact with Gus once and for all, but our little relationship was not over yet. Superintendent Carpenter, when he went to the FBI with my tape of Gus's threats, was told not to do anything yet, but by the end of June he was ready to move on Gus. While I was in protective custody my department took me down to the Suffolk County D.A.'s office, where we phoned Gus and taped the conversation. I told Gus I had the $25,000 and tried to arrange a meet. But he was cute. Either the feds had tipped him off or he smelled a rat, because he was not his usual co-operative self.

"Good to hear it, Jerry, good to hear it. It'll make my people very happy."

"So where can I meet you? Redstone Shopping Center?"

"Jesus, Jerry, no, nowhere near my house."

"Where then?"

"Thing is, it's been so long, I'm scared. These guys are not too happy about the delay, I gotta tell you."

"Come by my house, how about that? I'm not worried."

There was a long silence at Gus's end.

"I'll send someone by, Jerry, I'll have a guy pick it up."

"Gus, you crazy? How will I know? I tell you, I'm not giving this money to anyone but you."

"No can do."

"Then you aren't going to see the money. It's as simple as that."

"Jerry, I'm scared, you know, I'm scared. I'm taking off."

Gus was true to his word. He blew town so fast even his wife didn't see him go, and he did not reappear in Boston until nearly two years later. I had my own theory about his flight, but my department insisted on going by the book. They brought me to the district court in Cambridge and had me swear out a warrant for Gus's arrest, even though at that point I just wanted to drop the whole thing. That warrant would ultimately create another interesting story when Gus made his reappearance. But in the meantime I had more than a crazy stool pigeon to worry about—my own department now started stepping up its investigation.

The Depositors Trust Company, Medford, Massachusetts.

The optician's shop next door to the bank.

Brigham's ice cream parlor, corner of High Street and Governor's Ave.

The rear of the bank, as it appears today.

92

The scene greeting bank employees on Tuesday morning.

WBZ TV

The rifled safety deposit boxes.

The torched bank safe.

WBZ TV

The dynamited hole in the roof, as seen from the floor of the vault.

WBZ TV

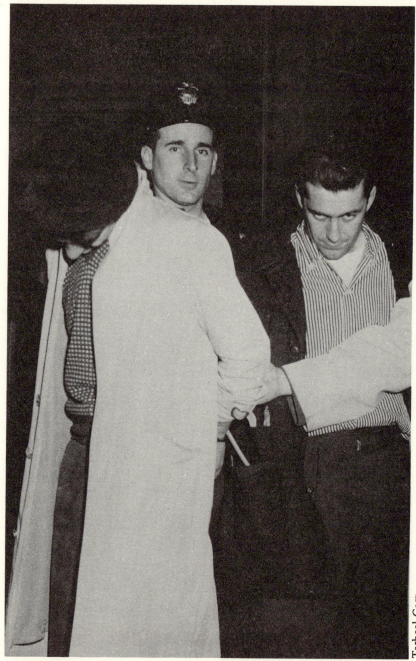

Jerry Clemente (rear) after apprehending two liquor store robbers in 1960.

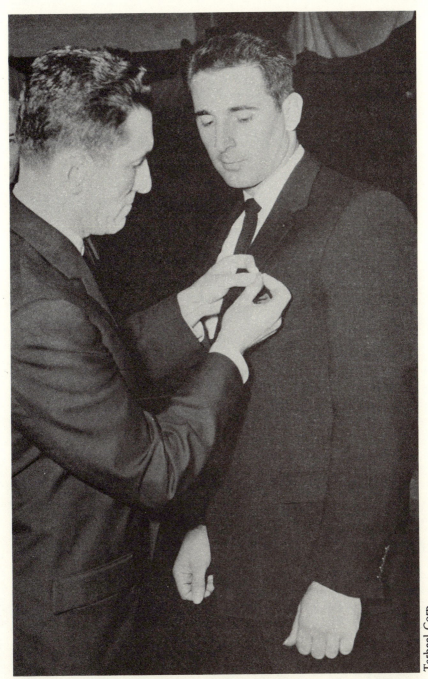

Tarheel Corp.

Better days: Jerry Clemente receiving his medal of valor from the Medford city manager in 1961.

Medford Police Station, only two blocks away from the Depositors Trust Company.

Tarheel Corp.

Joe Bangs (left) and Jerry Clemente in Florida in 1981.

After the shooting: Tommy's barn on Pleasant Street in Medford.

The Medford Mercury

State Police Detective Thomas Spartichino (center) emerges after investigating the attempted murder of Joe Bangs, October 16, 1984.

The Medford Mercury

Bangs on the stand during Doherty's trial—the first of many appearances as a witness.

The Medford Mercury

The Medford Mercury

Debbie O'Malley, Joe Bangs's girlfriend, testifies at Tommy Doherty's trial.

Tommy's house on Pleasant Street.

The Medford Mercury

WBZ TV

Tommy listens to testimony during his trial.

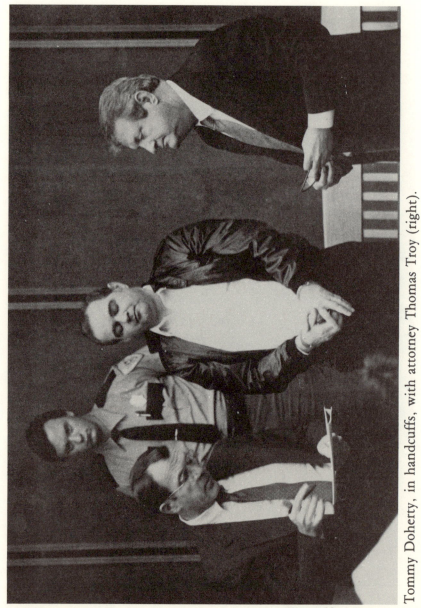

The Medford Mercury

Tommy Doherty, in handcuffs, with attorney Thomas Troy (right).

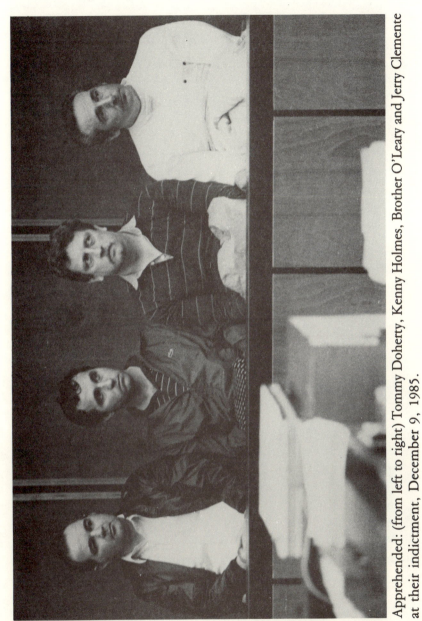

The Medford Mercury

Apprehended: (from left to right) Tommy Doherty, Kenny Holmes, Brother O'Leary and Jerry Clemente at their indictment, December 9, 1985.

Brother O'Leary (left) and Kenny Holmes listening to pretrial motions.

UPI/Bettman Newsphotos

The trial: Jerry Clemente makes a point to his attorney, Marty
Weinberg.

Jurors visit the Depositors Trust Company near the beginning of Clemente's trial.

Jurors view the vault.

112

Bangs points out Clemente as his testimony begins.

WBZ TV

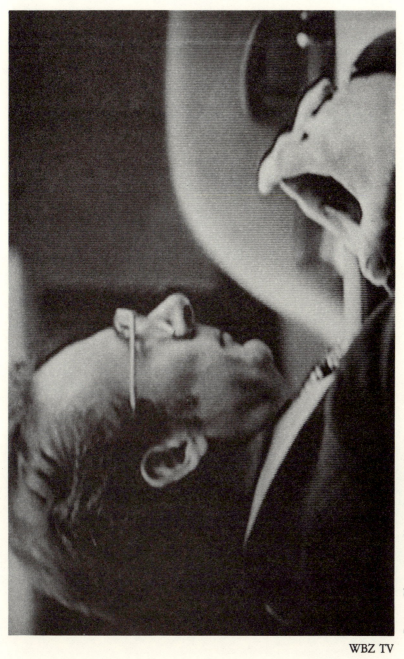

WBZ TV

Jerry Clemente listens to Bangs's testimony.

Barbara Hickey on the stand.

The Medford Mercury

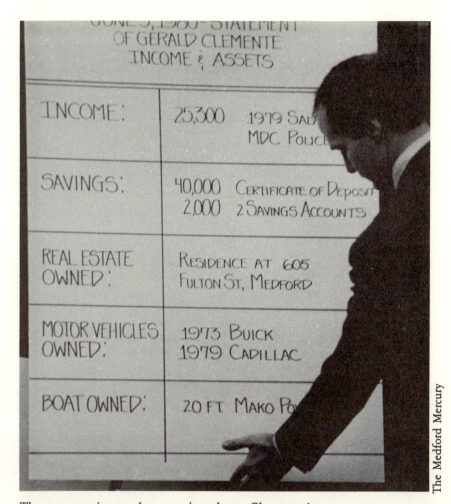

The prosecution makes a point about Clemente's assets.

The Medford Mercury

Judge Robert Barton reads Barbara Hickey's telling note while she looks on from the stand.

Jerry Clemente awaits the verdict, March 18, 1986.

UPI/Bettman Newsphotos

6

A Unique Situation

When my superiors suggested on Tuesday evening that my family and I go into protective custody, they did not give us much time to pack—by eleven p.m. we were on our way to the Holiday Inn in Somerville, the next town over from Medford, where we would stay for one night before being escorted by state troopers to a safe house the following morning. Agreeable as I was to protective custody, I was not happy with the control the Metropolitan Police would now have over my actions. The incident with the three Metropolitan cops made me suspect that people in my own department with deep and long-standing animosities towards me were using my position as a suspect to step up their efforts to get rid of me. I began to worry that not only were men of my own rank and lower after me, but my superiors as well. Soon it became obvious. From now on I was going to have a double fight: one to keep myself from being caught for the heist, and another to keep my job. I was going to have to play the role of an innocent man, acting outraged at what I pretended was only innuendo, when all along I knew that these men's suspicions were true.

When we arrived at the hotel Tom Keough handed me a written order, signed by Carpenter and witnessed by Keough himself, commanding me to take a polygraph.

"We'll escort you to Scientific Security tomorrow at one o'clock," he said.

"Tomorrow? What the hell kind of notice is that?"

"Jerry, I'm just following orders myself."

"How do I even know this is legal?"

"If Carpenter's doing it, it's legal, you know that. Besides, you're entitled to consult an attorney."

"By tomorrow morning? It's nearly midnight. This is all bullshit, you know that, don't you?"

Keough shrugged. He was a decent guy who was only doing what his superior told him. But I had my role to play.

"So the feds got to Carpenter, did they?"

Keough pointed to a line in the order: *The FBI has shown us enough evidence to convince us that you may have been involved in the burglary of the Depositors Trust Company.*

"Because of that," Keough said, "Carpenter feels a polygraph is advisable."

"Ah, cut the crap. If they have enough evidence then why the hell don't they indict me, answer me that?"

This was my standard question, my way of challenging suspicion. Keough couldn't answer because he knew as well as I that the force wanted to give me the shaft. Both he and I recognized that there was a game being played here. We all had our roles, and Keough's was that of the sympathetic superior officer who could do nothing for me. But one thing I knew I could count on from the superintendent was honesty. He was as straight as a slide rule. If he was going to get somebody out he was going to do it by the book, I knew that. He wasn't going to make it easy for me, but he wasn't going to stab me in the back either. So I signed the order.

But right then I had even more pressing concerns: I had to call Barbara Hickey. The decision to enter protective custody had been reached so quickly I did not have an opportunity to call her until after we arrived at the hotel, so when I phoned her from the lobby I was worried about her reaction. Naturally she would feel she was also in danger, and given her temperament I did not expect her to take the news calmly. I was right. She went hysterical, hollering and swearing at me and threatening to come down to the hotel herself. I tried to calm her down, but she hung up on me. Worried she might do something drastic, I immediately phoned my father and asked for his help. He and my brother went down to her house. At first she wouldn't answer, but after my father persisted she opened the door and yelled at them for a while as they tried to explain the situation. She was more annoyed than scared, it seemed, and it made me wonder about our relationship. I didn't know what to expect from her. Was she going to be able to handle all this?

I spent a sleepless night trying to determine whether or not I was constitutionally required by the regulations of the department to take the lie detector test on such short notice and without the advice of an attorney. Knowing how straight Carpenter was, I had to assume it was legal. But I also knew what my lawyer had told me before, that if I did not take the test voluntarily the results could not be held against me. So why was Carpenter ordering me? The only conclusion I could reach was that he hoped I would refuse so that he could have me up on insubordination. It was a tough one to call. It was as if I were playing a high stakes poker game with nothing in my hand. I had to do a lot of bluffing.

Late as it was, I called the divorce lawyer who had advised me the day of the FBI visit. He said he was going to be in probate court in Salem, Massachusetts, the following morning and that I should meet him there, so at six a.m. I had one of the troopers drive me up there for a quick conference. He advised me the best he could, but without any time to research the matter he couldn't tell me much. He did say he would drive into Boston that afternoon and accompany me during the test.

When I got back to the hotel the troopers took us out to Moon Island, an island in Boston harbor connected to the mainland by a causeway, where the D.A. had a safe house. Located at the tip of the island, completely fenced in, and well-guarded by both state police and Metropolitan cops, it was very safe, but I didn't get much of a chance to appreciate it that morning; as soon as the brass heard I had an attorney

coming in that afternoon they moved the time of the test up
to eleven o'clock and whisked me into the city immediately.

When Carpenter ordered me to take the test he said that
its scope would be limited to my actions over the Memorial
Day weekend. He also led me to believe that the department
would use its usual polygraph examiner from Rhode Island,
a scientifically objective operator with no ties to the department or any of the investigative agencies, to conduct the test.
When I arrived at the Boston Offices of Scientific Security,
however, I was surprised to find an entirely different operator,
a guy named Edward McGrath. He began with a pretest interview that was incredibly long and detailed—and many of
the questions were well outside the scope of the weekend in
question. When we moved into the testing room he attached
the usual sensors to my palms and the big rubber band around
my chest that would feed the sensitive physical information
of my responses to the polygraph.

"OK," he said, "just relax."

"Hey, don't I have to sign a waiver?"

"I was told you signed one last night."

"That was an order, a command."

But McGrath ignored my argument. He was very business-
like and very FBI. My suspicions were up from the start, and
when we began the test, sure enough, his questions were all
over the place. He asked my about a big Dedham bank robbery in 1977, which Bucky Barrett had been involved in, and
various B&Es in the Boston area over the years. He mentioned
the incident with Gusmini's friends Oulette and Oldham that
had happened two years previously.

"I was told," I said, "that the scope of this test was only
the Memorial Day weekend. What's all this other shit?"

"Procedure."

"What are you talking about, procedure? Are you trying
to get a confession out of me or what?"

"You're procedurally required to answer every question,
that's all I can tell you."

I answered the questions because strategy demanded I do, but I knew something was fishy. The department was pulling out all the stops, and what was I going to do? During the test I stared at an electrical outlet opposite me and tried to empty my mind of everything. Every half-hour—the length of a side of a cassette tape—McGrath excused himself to get a drink of water. As soon as we were finished I went straight to Keough.

"Something's wrong here, Tom. I don't like it."

"What do you mean?"

"Why didn't we use the usual guy? Who's this McGrath anyway?"

"Carpenter introduced me to him yesterday. Said that—"

"Yesterday? Listen Tom, this guy's a fed, I can tell by the questions he's asking me. And to my mind, he was taping me. That can't be legal."

Keough got on the phone and discovered that McGrath was indeed an ex-FBI agent.

"As far as I'm concerned this whole thing is invalid," I said. "I was ordered to take it, I didn't sign a waiver, and he asked questions outside of that weekend. The whole thing's a farce."

"So what are you worried about?"

I looked at him levelly.

"That's exactly what I want to know."

Keough shrugged. I knew he felt caught between a rock and a hard place.

"Take a message to Carpenter," I said. "If he's so concerned about getting the truth, tell him I have a little story of my own to tell. Dan Gately, Jake O'Brien and Tony LaConti were spying on me, hanging outside the house of a friend of mine while I was on my private time. I chased them down on the Revere Beach Parkway and the assholes had the balls to tell me they were looking at the site of an accident Gately had had in the area months ago. Four o'clock in the fucking morning and they're out looking at accident sites, can you believe that? Well, I'm officially complaining."

"Officially, Jerry?"

"Officially."

Two can play this game, I thought.

Physically, mentally and emotionally exhausted, I asked to be taken back to the safe house so I could get some sleep, but I received yet another order from Internal Affairs for one more written day-by-day description of my movements over the crucial weekend. I did so. By then I was bullshit. Let the department do what it wanted, I said to myself, I was on safe ground. And though I was right—that the polygraph couldn't be legally used against me—I didn't know that McGrath would become a key figure in the hearings the department would eventually use to bust my ass. When he appeared in those hearings with meticulously detailed "notes," I knew that somewhere there was a tape that I had been conned into making. But the department, because of the media attention and the fact that I was a captain, was concerned with its image. Embarrassed at having a captain among its ranks who had been the object of an investigation, it wanted to cleanse its image at my expense.

Now the obvious question is: Who could blame them? What right had I, a crooked cop, to expect fair treatment? After all, I was guilty of the crime; I had violated the public trust. But remember: as long as a criminal remains uncaught, he acts as if he is innocent. He thinks he is fully justified using all of the resources of the American legal system to avoid getting nailed for flagrantly illegal acts. He thinks that if someone else bends the rules, he has a right to complain. He works on a double standard that his lack of conscience prevents him from recognizing. That was my frame of mind at the time.

The rest of the week was equally hectic. While my wife and son stayed at the safe house, the guards ferried me to the D.A.'s office, Metropolitan headquarters and Cambridge District Court, taking care of the Gusmini business and giving me a hard time. I also kept in touch with Tommy by phone. He told me that another Medford cop had tried to extort him, telling Tommy that Howie Winters of the Winter Hill gang had sent him to collect $50,000 from Tommy. Tommy reported the cop to his superiors and they took action immediately. Blinded by my own false feelings of innocence, I wondered why I hadn't received the same support.

After a week I'd had enough of their surveillance. I was getting cabin fever, so I told them I was leaving. They told me they could not be responsible for my safety, but I knew that even Gusmini was long gone by then. Besides, my own department had given me more shit than he had. I wanted to be back on my own turf.

Compared to June, the month of July was a breeze. The heat cooled off and, without having to work, I had some time to attend to business. Through Bangs, I got the name of a good lawyer, Marty Weinberg, from Bucky Barrett. I paid the lawyer a $5,000 retainer towards future legal complications. If further money was needed, Joe assured me, Bucky would provide funds from the stash. Why not just get me my share? I felt like asking, but I knew that Bucky had had his own heat to deal with. I also filed an amended report with Internal Affairs when I remembered the peanut truck incident of May 23. I kept after Keough as well, hounding him to make sure Carpenter confronted Gately and his pals about their tailing me. On August 8, forty-eight days after I had been relieved of duty, I returned to work.

I returned as a captain, but for two months I was not allowed to perform my normal duties. Confined to a desk in HQ, kept out of uniform, I could not work overtime or drive a cruiser. But as it became clear that neither the FBI nor the state police had a case against me, the department was forced to restore me to my former position. In fact, I received a better job—I was assigned the captaincy of the Metropolitan Old Colony station in South Boston, a job that suited me better because I now worked days. It looked like I was emerging from the game a winner.

The probe against Gusmini continued. The Metropolitan Police asked the state police for help in locating him, but he had completely disappeared. He had not shown up at his house or his nightclub since my taped conversations in the D.A.'s office, and his wife said she had no idea where he had gone.

As a result of my complaint, Superintendent Carpenter confronted Gately, LaConti and O'Brien, who had all filed reports saying that they had seen me at Barbara Hickey's house during my on-duty time. Face-to-face with Carpenter, however, LaConti and O'Brien backed down, saying that they had not actually seen me. How did they know, then? Carpenter asked. Common knowledge, they replied. Carpenter blew his top. They were the ones who should be under investigation, he yelled, for filing false reports. Carpenter wanted me badly, but he knew that these three, by ganging up on me and trying to get me ousted the easy way, were in fact entrenching my position. Relying on hearsay and petty rivalry would only damage Carpenter's case in the long run. He wanted to do it right. Of the three of them, only Gately stuck by his charges, and only Gately would ever be called to testify against me.

Looking back on the whole affair now, I can see the situation involving these three men, and others in the department who didn't like me, much more clearly. People tend to lump police together, tarring them with the same brush of corruption or painting them all as white knights, but the fact is that, as in any job, every employee is different. There are good cops and bad cops. There are humane cops and there are ballbusters. But there are as many different kinds of policemen as there are kinds of people, and the relationships between them are often complex. I was a corrupt cop, but I had a better record, in some respects, than other cops who were perfectly straight. Many of the cops who hated me and wanted me out did so because they thought I had robbed a bank and stolen civil service exams—and they were right.

But often their animosity had more elaborate roots; often it resulted from the kind of personality conflict that is very common in public service jobs with internal competition, the kind of conflict that festers over years of rivalry. In my game with my department, my plan was to prove that personalities, not facts, were condemning me. I wanted my superiors to think I was innocent and harassed.

There were certainly enough personality conflicts to point to. I had a lot of problems, for example, with what police call bounty hunters, the cops that make every arrest they can, regardless of the circumstances, so that the resulting court appearances make them a substantial amount in overtime. These guys have the kind of hardassed attitude that antagonizes the public, and they never show the compassion that I feel a good police officer has to have in certain situations. Now, it may sound funny to hear me, a convicted bank burglar, talking about what makes a good policeman. But the fact is, whenever I had to deal with people, I always tried to do so in a humane fashion. It was as if I had two lives—one on the job, one off. Life is not always black and white.

I was always knocking heads with bounty hunters. In 1974, for example, two patrolmen under me arrested a woman on a default warrant, which ordinarily meant that she would not be eligible for bail. But the whole procedure was complicated by the fact that the woman had a six-week-old baby and no one to look after it. If she were not bailed she would have had to be brought, with the infant, to the "tombs," the city jail cells downtown that, to say the least, are not a pleasant place for anyone, never mind a baby. As the warrant had been issued in the neighboring Essex County, I called the clerk of court there and explained the situation, asking if there was a possibility of getting bail for this woman. It seemed to me the humane thing to do. The clerk said OK, so I left orders for the patrolmen to proceed to Nahant police station, where the woman and the baby were located. But when they got there they refused to let the woman be bailed. They brought her back to Revere, where I was stationed, and I got into a very heated argument with them in front of the station. I made it very clear to them that as long as I was in charge I would run the station my way, not theirs. I tried to impress their lack

of compassion on them and I had them return to Nahant for
bail. These guys, I knew, didn't like me, but I was not going
to allow them to undermine my authority.

From that point on these guys made a point of breaking
my balls. One day I was conducting an in-service training session, a short period of training conducted by the officer-in-
charge that we often had just before roll call. That particular
evening my topic was driving under the influence, and I made
the suggestion that not everybody caught driving under the
influence need be arrested. A guy who wrapped his car around
a tree, for example, and had done no harm to anyone but
himself could, it seemed to me, be sent home in a cab with
a stern warning. In my view, that guy would have suffered
enough. One of these patrolmen disputed the point vociferous-
ly. Now I don't mind someone disagreeing with me; in this
case I could even have been wrong, as the latest studies on
drunk driving seem to indicate. But his motive for disagreeing was simple animosity, a motive that was confirmed when
he returned to the station fifteen minutes after roll call with
a DWI collar. He had deliberately searched out the bust so
that he could show me up.

This guy was not an exception. A lot of cops go after busts
for no reason other than simple malice. Or they have bills due
at the end of the month, so they go after every cracked tail-
light, every broken muffler, hoping that the driver will have
a drink or two on him, warranting a ticket—which means a
court appearance and overtime pay for the arresting officer.
A study that examined the correlation between time of the
month and the number of tickets issued would be interesting,
and it wouldn't surprise me at all to see the rate go up as the
end of each month approached.

I never had any sort of patience for this sort of behavior,
and I didn't pretend not to notice. "Whose life are you going
to screw up tonight?" I'd yell at known bounty hunters as
they started their shift. Naturally these guys saw me as soft.
They saw compassion as a weakness. And they saw nothing

wrong with putting an innocent man or woman through the legal mill, at the cost of perhaps thousands of dollars in legal fees and lost time, simply so that they could collect their sixty-buck court-appearance fee. I didn't like these guys, and they knew it. So animosity was definitely there, and when these kind of guys heard rumors about my involvement in the bank job and the sale of stolen civil service exams, they resented me even more. They saw me advancing quickly up the hierarchy of the Metropolitan Police, they disliked me personally, and so they did what they could to bust my balls.

But I had more than bounty hunters to worry about; intra-departmental bickering concerned me only insofar as it threatened my job, because now I was fighting on two fronts —one to keep my past under wraps, and the other to keep from being fired or demoted.

When I returned to work in August of 1980, things were pretty quiet, though early in September, while still confined out of uniform to a desk in HQ, I did get a three-page list of questions from Superintendent Carpenter as part of the on-going Internal Affairs investigation. Significantly, the definition of the investigation had broadened. The Memorial Day weekend was no longer at issue; now my "fitness to serve as a police officer" was under review. The questions asked specifically about my relationship with Barbara Hickey and the performance of my duties as watch commander. I suspected that, unable to substantiate the rumors of my involvement in the robbery, the department was trying to nail me on other grounds, but I meticulously answered the questions with the help of my attorney and returned them to Carpenter five days later. I had always received good evaluations, and I knew that my competence as a commander could not be seriously in question. The questions had to be a smoke screen.

I assumed my captaincy in South Boston in October, and for almost six months I heard nothing. In November I had my regularly scheduled evaluation by Deputy Superintendent John McDonough, who said I was a "competent, efficient supervisor imbued with a common sense approach to most situations." I continued doing my job and assumed that Carpenter's probe had come to nought. He couldn't nail me, I thought, pleased with myself. I had him outfoxed.

Around the beginning of 1981, when rumors of Carpenter's retirement started circulating, I breathed a little easier. And when McDonough became acting superintendent after Carpenter's retirement in March, I really relaxed. McDonough had always given me the impression that he was on my side, even though he used to say half-jokingly that when he looked over his shoulder he saw me coming. So I was surprised when, within a matter of days after Carpenter had left, McDonough sent me another list of questions concerning Gusmini, the bust of Oldham and Oulette in 1978 and Jimmy Tortelli. The questions contained direct references to statements I had made during the pretest interview I had had with McGrath prior to the polygraph. I went to McDonough immediately.

"I'm sorry, Jerry, this is a situation I inherited."

"Inherited? I haven't heard anything for six months!"

"Carpenter was pursuing the investigation."

"Investigation of what, the robbery or my competence as a police officer?"

"Well, they're...you know, tied together."

"Don't bullshit me, John. You evaluated me in November. You said I was doing a good job."

This was my stance—I was a good cop under suspicion. McDonough tapped his tabletop with his fingernails.

"Look, Jerry—we have a unique situation here, and we don't quite know how to handle it."

"So?"

"So don't worry about it. We have certain procedures to observe."

Just what McGrath had said. But I took McDonough at his word and answered the questions. I prefaced my answers with a long explanation of the circumstances surrounding the polygraph, done with the aid of my attorney. I made it clear that many of the statements were obtained under false pretences. I also tried to get copies of the test results and questions. I had made arrangements with the attorney general of Tennessee to take the test down there and, assuming I passed, use the new results to contest the Metropolitan Police's polygraph. Obviously I needed the exact same questions for the comparison to be valid, but McDonough wouldn't give them to me. In the meantime my attorney was telling me that if I had had him as counsel in June I would never have had to take the test in the first place. That didn't make me feel any better. My grip on the situation was beginning to slip. I was starting to scramble.

McDonough continued to reassure me, telling me he was simply following procedure as he kept the wheels of the investigation turning. I have to hand it to him, he did his job well. In May he took the first big step towards getting me out, though he kept telling me otherwise; he instructed me to make a lengthy deposition in the presence of two attorneys, my own and the department's. The deposition was a long, courtroom-type interview with direct questioning, cross-examination and fourteen exhibits, including reports, letters and department memoranda. The deposition, which took place on June 4, 1981, almost a year to the day since my initial confrontation with the FBI, was incredibly detailed. The Metropolitan attorney, Lawrence Ball, grilled me on my background, the performance of my duties, my relationship with Barbara Hickey, the FBI's visit to my house, Gusmini, the peanut truck incident, the polygraph and other events stretching back in time. When typed up, the deposition ran over 120 pages, representing five hours of testimony. My lawyer made the appropriate objections at the appropriate times, but because we were not in a court of law—or even a hearing for that matter—they were only cosmetic. At the outset Ball pointed out that any evidence gleaned from the interview could not be held against me in a criminal proceeding, but of course there was less at stake here than criminal charges. My job was on the line. And yet I had McDonough's assurance that the whole thing was only procedure.

In August the acting superintendent dropped his bombshell: I received a letter from the commissioner notifying me that I was to appear at the end of the month before a commission hearing to determine if I should be punished for violations of departmental rules and regulations. The letter detailed fifteen specific charges centered around three areas: spending on-duty time at Barbara Hickey's house, neglecting my duties as watch commander, and communicating confidential information to Gusmini after the Oldham-Oulette bust back in 1978. After keeping me in the dark McDonough had done what even Carpenter had not dared to do. He had taken action to get me demoted or fired, and I was bullshit.

The hearings were detailed and extensive. Spread out over five months—September 1981 to January 1982—they involved twenty exhibits and thirty witnesses, including Barbara Hickey, Daniel Gately, Tommy Doherty, FBI Agent Neil Cronin, former superintendent Carpenter, Thomas Keough, a variety of Metropolitan and Medford cops and myself. There were days and days of testimony on incidents that either never happened or occurred with total innocence: whether or not I had really attended to that peanut truck crash; whether my cruiser had or had not been outside Barbara Hickey's house; whether or not I had revealed confidential information to Gusmini after the bust of his associates. The prosecution argued hard for a major demotion. My own attorneys, confident of success, picked apart the allegations. One of them said to me during the hearing: "If this were a court of law, Jerry, this case would have been thown out a long time ago."

But we were not in a court of law. The hearing was a battle of wills, mine against the department's. I knew the odds were not in my favor, so it didn't surprise me when the hearing officer ruled in favor of the prosecution. In February 1982 I was moved back to HQ on Somerset Street, and on April 5 Commissioner Terrence Geoghegan officially informed me that he had found just cause to discipline me. "Your actions," he wrote, "compel a demotion of more than one grade." He demoted me to the rank of sergeant, effective April 9.

Any demotion is a humiliation. A double demotion is particularly demeaning, especially for a man who has served for more than two decades. My punishment for the bank robbery had begun. By April I was on "line of duty" disability—on March 1 a file cabinet had tumbled down on top of me and thrown my back out—so I was at least spared the indignity of reporting as a sergeant under men I had previously commanded.

I appealed the decision at once to the Civil Service Commission of Massachusetts and, after much going back and forth, I was granted a hearing the following July. Barbara Hickey, for reasons I'll get to later, refused to testify for me at the civil service hearing, but I don't think her testimony would have made any difference. The outcome was determined from the start and nothing was going to change it. We went through the same long routine again, many of the same witnesses, much of the same tired testimony, but my defense was fruitless. Edward McGrath, the polygraph operator who had grilled me two years previously, was allowed to testify about the pretest interview he had given me. He referred repeatedly to detailed "notes," culled no doubt from a surreptitious tape. I didn't have a chance.

As if I didn't have enough to worry about at this point, in September I got news that Vernon Gusmini, who had been on the lam for two years, had been arrested in a Florida hotel on charges unrelated to my extortion complaint. The last thing I needed was that stool pigeon coming back to sing, but because my complaint against him for attempted extortion was still outstanding, the Metropolitan Police decided to send someone down to collect him. Meanwhile, the people at the Middlesex County D.A.'s office, thinking Gus could provide information on the Depositors Trust heist, decided they wanted to talk to him as well.

The D.A.'s office dispatched State Police Lieutenant Tom Spartichino to Florida; my department sent detective Joe McCain. Now, there is no love lost between the Metropolitan Police and the Massachusetts State Police. Politically, the two forces have always been at odds, an antagonism that has been strengthened over the course of a number of tough gubernatorial elections between Massachusetts' current governor, Michael Dukakis, whom the Metropolitan Police have consistently supported, and Edward King, always the darling of the staties. The two organizations have frequently found it tough working together, and the pursuit of Gusmini was no exception. The extradition process started off fine, with Spartichino and McCain meeting amiably enough at Logan Airport, but almost immediately a bizarre coincidence occurred.

Amazingly, I was flying to Florida the same day. I had arranged a fishing trip with my friend George McGarrity (who, ironically, is a state trooper himself) a number of weeks beforehand. I was to fly out on Friday, and George, who had a golf tournament to complete in New Hampshire, was to join me on Monday. When I got out to the airport, lo and behold, whom did I see but Spartichino and McCain. We all ignored each other. Spartichino, who had been working on the bank case for two years, was suspicious at once. He thought I was going down to Florida to "take care of" Gusmini myself. He pointed out his fears to McCain. McCain defended me. An argument ensued, and the tension level rose.

The argument continued once the two men got to Florida, but McCain, who had the warrant, won out. After checking that Gus was indeed in a West Palm Beach jail, the two men had words, and Spartichino flew back to Boston with the understanding that McCain would follow shortly afterwards and meet the state police at Logan Airport, where he would hand Gus over.

In the meantime, another Metropolitan detective, John Picardi, flew to Miami, rented a car and drove up to West Palm Beach, where he met McCain and Gusmini. My department, more out of rivalry with the troopers than anything else, wanted to keep Gus to themselves, interviewing him and assessing his relations with me before the state police could get their hands on him. So McCain and Picardi, after booking reservations on every flight to Boston out of West Palm Beach Airport to throw the state police off, drove Gusmini back to Massachusetts, getting lost on the way.

The state police waited and waited at Logan. When McCain didn't show up, they raised hell. My department, as it would, remained closemouthed. They weren't giving anything away to their rivals. Naturally, the D.A. thought that, at the worst, Gusmini was going to disappear, or, at best, that the Metropolitan cops were shielding me from testimony that might implicate me in the bank job. Now, the events prior to this incident make it clear that my department was not interested in protecting me from anyone; it was after my ass itself. But there was no convincing the state police of that, so by the time they did get Gusmini back in their clutches they grilled him for days on the bank and on the circuitous journey from Florida to Massachusetts. Gus, canny as he was, played right into their hands, saying he was scared for his life the whole way. He also went through the whole false business of the Mob being after him, stuff that I knew would never stand up in court.

In October the D.A. convened a grand jury to investigate whether McCain and Picardi had obstructed justice. The jury declined to charge them. The D.A. also brought Gus and me before another grand jury, which indicted Gus for attempted extortion. I had to explain why I was out at Logan Airport the same day that McCain and Spartichino were flying down to get Gus; after all, my motives were under suspicion. Fortunately I was able to prove that I had booked my ticket for that day before Gus's whereabouts were known. I was in the clear.

But the prospect of Gus's trial was unsettling to me, especially as the demotion appeal was still going on. I knew that if the trial proceeded I would have to appear on the stand and testify about the bank and about civil service exams. While I was certain that Gus didn't know anything incriminating about me, I did not want that can of worms opened in court, so I decided to file an affidavit saying I planned to take the fifth if I was ever called to testify at Gus's trial. So the case was dropped.

In the meantime my appeal on my demotion came to a close. On January 18, 1983, the hearing officer officially recommended that the Civil Service Commission vote to affirm the previous hearing. Since September, when a police-appointed doctor had ordered me back to work, I had been dipping into the hundreds of sick days I had accrued over the years. Those days lasted until May 1983, when I retired. I had not worked in over a year.

So the unique situation had finally been resolved, the battle completed. I was the loser this time, but the war continued. One layer of the complex slice of events created by the robbery had been revealed, but it was only a surface layer. Much was happening beneath the surface during those years that had nothing to do with my professional life and a lot to do with paranoia, fear and greed.

7

A Question of Shares

By the end of the summer of 1980, as the heat cooled off and my life returned to something resembling a normal pattern, my mind gradually freed itself from worry and began considering other important matters. The newspapers were still rife with speculation and innuendo, the FBI still pursued its investigations vigorously, and the Metropolitan Police's prosecution of me still lay ahead, but as far as the robbery was concerned I was now confident that, barring disaster, I would not get caught. It's not that I wasn't still a suspect; people talked about me and the heist in the same breath, sometimes even to my face, but I never got defensive. I took the attitude that if anyone could prove my involvement, let him. In the meantime I was secure.

But within the gang, other dramas were developing between individuals and concerning the gang as a whole, including the possibility of another burglary even more audacious and profitable than the Depositors Trust. It was only natural that, given our first success, we should try for a repeat performance, and we all kept our eye out for another hit. But my main concern for the first year after the heist was not the money I might get in the future but the cash I was due from the past. I still had visions of millions of dollars' worth of diamonds and pearls and gold coins strewn across Joe Bangs's cellar; I could still hear Bucky and Kenny itemizing those pink diamonds and black pearls and jewel-studded rings as they estimated the haul as high as $25 million; but I still had not seen a penny more than my cash share. I wanted what was coming to me.

Even if Bucky could get only a fifth of what he thought the gold and jewels were worth, there should still have been enough to make us all millionaires, and I for one was getting impatient. He had been sitting on the stash for over three months now, and, while I did not expect him to be able to convert it to cash overnight, I certainly did not want the wait to stretch into years. Though Joe had always assured me that Bucky was honorable, I knew from experience that the longer these kind of delays were allowed to drag on, the greater the chances of something going wrong. And I wasn't the only one concerned. Tommy and Brother, I knew, were also getting restless, and even Joe got pissed at Bucky from time to time, though his anger was probably staged.

So in September I started bugging Joe about arranging a meeting. I had still not seen Bucky since the heist, and I argued that enough time had elapsed for us to be able to get together without suspicion. Joe stalled for a while, but in October he did get us all together at a bar in Cambridge. The only gang member absent was Kenny, who had blown town for reasons of his own. Though the atmosphere was a little tense, there was also a sense of camaraderie at being back together. Brother cracked a few jokes, loosening us up, but I got right down to business.

"So, Bucky, what about the gold and jewels?"

"I got them stashed."

"When do we get our shares?"

Bucky sipped his beer and looked at each of us in turn.

"Look, I don't know about you guys, but I've been taking some serious heat."

"And we haven't?"

"The FBI has been on my case big time. I'm still on parole, you know. They're watching my every fucking move."

"So?"

"So I can't get to the fucking stuff. Believe me, I want my share as much as you guys want yours, but it would be suicide to try to move any of it at this point. You talk about admissi-

ble evidence—all it takes is one little thing, one fucking ring
or watch or necklace to fall into the wrong hands, and bang,
I'm screwed. And with my record, that'd be it, you know what
I'm saying? You guys gotta appreciate that.''

The others looked at me. Being the most calm, the most
level-headed, I had been tacitly designated spokesman.

"Look, Bucky, we appreciate that, we really do. But you
can't blame us for wanting what's coming to us. It's been four
fucking months.''

Bucky threw his hands in the air.

"Hey, you don't think I know that? Answer me this—have
you guys been spending your money?''

We all shook our heads.

"My point exactly. You don't spend money that's still hot
and you don't go pawning hot items that could get you involved in compromising situations. Like I always said, you
can't be too careful.''

"So when *do* you move it?'' Tommy said.

"Listen, you guys know this—I got my own jewelry store
in Lynn, I got my own smelter. Couple weeks or so and I'm
going to start melting down some of the gold. I'll refashion
it into new pieces, stud them with diamonds and whatever,
and sell them out of my store. Thing is, it'll take some time.
I also got some connections in Florida, gem people I know,
who can do some moving for me. They'll want a cut, of course,
but as soon as the FBI's off my back I'll be getting down to
business.''

"A cut?'' Brother said. "How much will these friends of
yours be looking for?''

"Couple grand, whatever. Nothing really when you consider how much we got.''

"When you consider how much we got,'' Brother said, "it's
pretty fucking amazing we haven't seen a nickel of our
shares.''

"Don't worry, you will.''

Bucky's rap was a tapdance, a softshoe he would shuffle
quite a few times during that coming year, but for a while

it was convincing. He did have a long record, after all, so he couldn't take any chances. We spent the rest of the meeting comparing notes on FBI surveillance and alibis. Joe plugged me for information about Barbara—he knew about her flap when I went into protective custody—but I told him everything was cool. And it was. How long it would stay that way was another matter.

As soon as I got out of protective custody I told Barbara that she should expect a visit from the FBI. Tell them nothing, I counseled her; after my own little brush with them at my home and the fiasco of the polygraph I felt that they could not be trusted. But I wasn't worried either. At this point in the investigation I knew that the feds were working on the theory that whoever robbed the bank had been inside for three straight days and nights. All Barbara had to do was tell the truth and I would be free of a good deal of suspicion. But even if the investigators did piece the truth together, Barbara's statements of my presence at her house would still make it look as though I had not altered my usual routine. My alibi, I felt, was strong. Not ironclad, perhaps, but strong enough to keep me free from an indictment. And that was all I needed.

At the beginning of July I arranged for a private investigator from my attorney's office to ask Barbara a series of questions regarding the Memorial Day weekend. With her full cooperation he recorded her answers and had her sign a statement of their veracity. My attorney wanted something we could use to combat the FBI's investigation. But when the feds visited her in August she gave them nothing that I hadn't given them already. The times she said I visited her were the times I had indicated. What's more, she had a comprehensive calendar—a diary, in fact—that she had checked carefully before they questioned her. She kept this calendar religiously, recording everything that happened to her, and she never showed it to anyone, not even her closest friends. When the feds asked to have a look at it, she refused to show it to them.

That same month Barbara made the first of what would be three grand jury appearances relating to my involvement in the heist. In that first appearance, before a federal grand jury, she told the truth. Her lawyer, there at my expense, had the private investigator's statement with him. Attorneys are not allowed into the courtroom during grand jury proceedings, but the person being questioned may leave the room at any time to consult with his attorney outside. Barbara left the room twenty-seven times and took her Fifth Amendment right against self-incrimination thirty-three times. I was satisfied.

When Joe Bangs later testified at my trial that I told him I had confused Barbara Hickey to the point where she didn't know she was lying, he was lying himself. Anyone who knew Barbara knew there was no confusing her. She was very sure of herself and very meticulous about that calendar. But she knew what she was doing. When the second grand jury subpoenaed it, she claimed it was lost, though not before she had written out a schedule of the times I had spent at her home. At my trial she claimed she had perjured herself. She said she lied to the grand jury. I felt betrayed because my memory of those times was that they were correct. Of course, the diary was no longer around to settle the matter.

But Barbara was only one witness in that first grand jury investigation, which was extensive. The many subpoenas handed down included ones for a number of Medford cops, the man who owned the optical shop next door to the bank, bank employees and, in January 1981, my wife Mary. I was not called because under the rules of the federal court you cannot be brought before a grand jury if you are the target of an investigation. Even so, the jury could not find enough evidence to hand down an indictment and adjourned without establishing anything conclusive. The newspapers continued printing their stories and the FBI continued its probe, but I was a step closer to never being caught.

But that grand jury proved to be a turning point for me in quite a different way; from then on I thought I noticed a clear change in Barbara Hickey's attitude towards me, a change that was very subtle at first, but one that grew so quickly that within the year we were finished with each other once and for all. I see now that what had been beneath the surface had finally been aired. There had always been warning signs that we were not right for each other. It may have been my imagination, but it seemed to me that after she testified on my behalf, I was buying more things for her.

I always was a provider. You name it and I bought it for her: car, refrigerator, television, washing machine, dryer. I bought sheds for her backyard and built an extension to her house. I paid all her bills, including hefty legal fees. I never breathed a word of the robbery to her; I was always extremely careful in that regard. But obviously she read the papers and listened to the rumors on the Metropolitan Police, so she knew I was a serious suspect. I began to think she was suspicious of me, so I became suspicious of her. Our relationship started to deteriorate. We started to argue more and more often. Like a fool I stuck around. In fact, for a short period during 1981 I actually moved in with her. Then the pressure really started—complaints about money, demands for attention and every day the same question: When was I going to get a divorce? She arranged appointments with lawyers and dragged me from pillar to post trying to impose her will on me, trying to make me do something I knew deep down I didn't want to do.

Even the lawyers could see I didn't want a divorce. I got to know one of them quite well and he told me repeatedly: "Don't do anything you don't want to do, Jerry." Unfortunately my state of mind was such that I allowed the relationship to continue. I had somehow gotten into that self-destructive loop that people in bad relationships find so hard to get out of, and the shriller she got, the less able I was to detach myself. But I would not get a divorce.

Then, towards the end of 1981, she did double duty for me. With a grant of immunity this time, she appeared again before a federal grand jury and again stuck to the facts. With immunity, I reasoned, she had absolutely no reason to lie.

Around the same time she appeared at the Metropolitan disciplinary hearings, testifying on my behalf. But it seemed to me that the more she appeared, the worse our relationship got. I felt as if I was supporting two families—hers and mine—and all I was getting out of it was a bad relationship and no support. It was getting to be too much. After living with her for six months, I moved out in November.

Around that time she refused to testify at the civil service hearing. As I've said, I don't think her failure to appear cost me anything in the long run, but at the time her decision was painful. I was at a point in the relationship where I knew I had to make a clean break once and for all, but habit kept me hanging in against my better judgement. One night in August I made a final pitch for her to testify. We were having dinner at a restaurant in Swampscott, a suburb north of Boston, and throughout the meal I argued with her, explaining how important her appearance at the hearing would be. As we finished the main course she looked me straight in the eye.

"Sure I'll testify," she said, "as long as you do the right thing."

"Meaning?"

"You know what I mean."

"Listen, we've been over all this before. I just can't waltz into a divorce, you know. I need some time on this."

"You've had plenty of time."

"Even the lawyer says I should wait until after the hearing."

"I know all about you and Frank," she said. "I know the games you're playing. You want him to stall me until afterwards and he's going along with you because you're big pals now."

"Hey, you introduced us."

"Yeah, and you charmed him like you charm everybody, and now he thinks I'm a bitch and you're the greatest thing since sliced bread."

She gave me as dirty a look as I'd ever received from her as the waiter put our dessert in front of us.

"You know," she said, "I know your friends. I know Joe Bangs and Doherty and all those guys."

"So you know them, big fucking deal. You threatening me?"

She said nothing.

"Go ahead, then," I yelled, "make it rough for them. See if I give a shit."

She pursed her lips and shook her head.

"Just do the right thing."

It was all I could do not to throw my dessert in her face. The dinner had been one long trial, one more big reason why I should have nothing to do with her. I wiped my mouth with my napkin, threw fifty bucks on the table to cover the bill and said:

"Have a nice walk home."

Even that wasn't the last straw. We managed to patch things up temporarily after that, but when we had another big argument over a car insurance bill she received in December, I blew my top. That was it. We just weren't going to get along. I walked out and didn't see her again until my trial in 1986. During those three years something must have happened, because by the time she testified at my trial she had reversed her testimony. She claimed in court that she had lied to the grand jury. I don't know why she did this about-face, but I couldn't help wondering if she was still angry at me.

And I certainly wasn't getting any richer waiting for my share. As the winter dragged on Bucky continued his softshoe and Joe his lame defense: "Don't worry about him," Joe kept saying, "he'll come through." But the rest of us were becoming skeptical and impatient. What was taking him so long? We started discussing Bucky's antics among ourselves, and talk of taking Bucky out even began to slip into the heated discussions. I had to do some heavy-duty persuading to keep the violence at the level of threats only. Apart from my aversion to violence, I also did not want Joe or Tommy or Brother doing something stupid and getting us all in trouble. At that point I still thought that all Bucky needed was a good kick in the pants. I still trusted him.

In March of 1981 my wife and I flew to Miami with a group of Boston policemen to participate in the city's St. Patrick's Day festivities. It was quite a bash. While we were there a friend of mine introduced me to a real estate broker who was in the middle of a big estate deal and had some condos to get rid of—quickly. But she was asking $150,000 each, when I had to be careful how much money I threw around. Jokingly I offered her fifty grand, and to my surprise she was interested. We hammered out a deal at $78,000, and just like that I was a Florida property owner.

Back in Boston Joe Bangs got hyper when I told him about the purchase, saying that it would create suspicion, claiming that I couldn't account for the money. But the fact was I used no Depositors Trust money for the buy; the deal was one I could have closed whether I had robbed a bank or not, and I was absolutely unworried what people thought. But my purchase opened the floodgates. Before I knew it the other guys were investing their proceeds like crazy. Tommy spruced up a tool rental business that he had operated on the fringe for years, and he bought more real estate in Medford, including a couple more houses on Pleasant Street, which he was fast turning into his own personal street. He would take out a loan, buy a house, fix it up and then borrow on that house in order to buy another so it didn't look like he was spending a lot of cash. Brother bought a big house in Tewksbury, putting it in his wife's name, and invested in a bar in Quincy with his brother. Joe turned his house into a mansion. He installed a big swimming pool, added rooms and built stables on the property, even though he had never ridden a horse in his life. He too invested in real estate. At one point he approached me about investing in a condominium conversion project in Somerville—the builders were looking for $50,000 each from five investors—but like many of Joe's deals it fell through. For my own part, I did not want to engage in any transactions that I couldn't have closed under normal circumstances. I did not want attention. And yet I was growing more confident all the time that we were not going to get caught.

None of us told the others where he hid the money—none of us, that is, except Brother, who foolishly kept his share buried behind Joe's aunt's house on Cape Cod along with Joe's bundle. Joe later stole $75,000 from him. Joe and Brother liked to spend, and to account for their wealth they would fly to Las Vegas or Atlantic City, buy thousands of dollars' worth of chips, and then cash them in as winnings after a couple of days of light betting. Making sure they got receipts, they paid taxes on the cash and came out looking like a couple of lucky guys.

But there is nothing like spending money to make you want more, and before long, as Bucky procrastinated and Joe made excuses, I began to consider new angles and new ways of making big bucks. The nature of greed is funny. When you have nothing, the thought of $175,000 is overwhelming, and you imagine that if you had that kind of cash you would be satisfied. But the reality is that you never have enough. If having nothing makes you dream of thousands, having thousands makes you dream of millions. And if you are a person in my position, a person who has lost his focus because of greed, you go about trying to make that dream a reality. For me, that reality developed towards the end of the summer of '81, when the idea for the next big heist came to me out of the blue with such obviousness that I wondered how I had not thought of it sooner.

I was browsing through the *Boston Herald* one day when I came across the annual list of names it prints of people who are due money from lapsed bank accounts and recently settled estates. In a flash it came to me: this money was all kept in a treasury vault on the twelfth floor of the McCormack Building in downtown Boston, a building that I had become increasingly familiar with through my visits there with various members of the Capitol Police, the force that guards the building. Since 1977 I had been checking out the building from time to time, picking locks and wandering the halls as I searched the rooms for civil service exams. With Tommy's help I had broken into the sophisticated safes and copied exams, but the thought of going after the big money in the state treasury there never occurred to me. Now I couldn't believe I'd missed it. I knew that a lot of state employees, thousands in fact, cashed their checks there. I knew we could count on several million dollars being in the vault.

When I told Joe he did his usual hyper, nuts-grabbing dance. He wanted to go straight into the building that night—and fuck the rest of the guys, he said. But I knew we needed the rest of the gang, not only because we needed the manpower and the cooperation, but also because I saw an opportunity to make Bucky come around on the gold bulk and jewels. If he got us our shares, I figured, I could cut him in on this job.

Joe and I staked out the building to see when the Brinks truck arrived and how security operated. A large double-bay garage with a platform was at the side of the building, and I knew the doors led into a freight elevator that could take us right to the twelfth floor. The Capitol Police had an ambulance out there and also kept a dozen or so large gray postal carts on the platform that would be perfect for ferrying the loot out of the vault, down the elevator and into a waiting truck backed up to the platform. That part, at any rate, looked easy, and when Joe and I discovered that the Brinks truck arrived on Wednesdays, we arranged a meeting with Tommy, Brother and Bucky.

The meeting took place at Joe's girlfriend's house, and by the time I got there a heated conversation was already underway. Brother was yelling at Bucky.

"So are you moving this stash or what? What's taking so fucking long?"

"I moved a little, a little. You can only move so fast, you know, and there are some expenses I gotta take care of first."

"Like what?"

"Like Frankie Sarducci wants more money. He was the wise guy who gave us permission to do the job, or don't you guys remember?"

"We already gave him a hundred grand."

"That was an installment."

"Bullshit."

"Besides," Joe said, "Sarducci's in the can."

"You're wrong, pal. Out on parole since last month. And even if he was still there, you don't think he wouldn't be running things?"

"Permission?" Brother fumed. "How the fuck do we need permission for something we already did?"

"Listen, Brother, this guy, this guy blows people's legs off for fun. No way am I gonna stiff him on what's due him. The gangs have been breathing down my neck and Sarducci called them off. The way it is with these guys, you pay them and they take care of you. You don't pay them and they take you out."

"That's it, that's your expenses?"

"No. I had to float some dough to my pals down in Florida for helping me with my alibi."

"So everybody gets a fucking piece except us, is that it?"

Brother stood up and pointed at Bucky. For once Joe was not defending Bucky.

"Look," I said, "let's cool down here. Even if you paid those guys a million bucks, that's only the tip of the iceberg, right?"

"Icebergs take a long time to melt," Bucky said. "You can't draw attention to yourself. I know it's going slow, but you guys gotta be patient."

Joe went over to a closet.

"Bucky, I got a little something I want to show you."

He pulled out a sawed-off shotgun.

"This is an interesting piece I picked up recently."

He fiddled with the works for a few seconds and returned the gun to the closet without a word. But the look on Bucky's face spoke volumes—he was scared shitless. I decided it was time to change the subject, so I introduced the treasury plan. Everybody was so excited that they forgot the beef with Bucky completely as I outlined what Joe and I had discovered.

"What about security?"

"There are two Capitol cops in there," I said, "and one of them is always asleep. The other is in a control room watching the alarm system and a couple of TV monitors. But not all the doors are bugged. I've got a master key that will get us in the back door. I have a key to the freight elevator. We'll be able to get to the twelfth floor no problem."

"Not everything'll be on that master key," Bucky said. "Not the security staff."

"I've been inside the locksmith's room," I said. "I got all the codes to the special locks and I can get into any fucking door in that building if we can bypass the alarm."

It was like the Depositors Trust all over again—the excitement, the planning, the dreams. The following week we went inside the building and looked around, wearing nylon stockings over our heads once we reached the twelfth floor because there were television cameras at the corners of the treasury that would be activated if we tripped an alarm. The wall opposite the elevator door was lined with tellers' windows, and we knew somehow we had to get behind those windows. The door beside the windows was bugged. Farther down was an unbugged door and, using my master key, we went inside. In that room was the door we had to get through. I took the number of the special security lock and returned to the hallway. Bucky had found an electrical room with a little box inside marked *door alarms*. He took a few notes and we left.

It was a few weeks before we were able to return, and in the meantime I did a lot of thinking. I wasn't fully certain that I wanted to involve myself any more deeply with guys like Bucky and Joe, whom I was increasingly inclined to distrust. When we did meet, I had a few words with Bucky at his car and got the same old spiel. When I noticed that Joe had neglected to bring Brother along, I mentioned it to him. Fuck Brother, he said. Brother was supposed to be Joe's friend, his partner. If Joe treated him in this way, how was he going to treat me?

But a job like this has its own momentum, the momentum of greed that keeps somebody like me hanging around with men I'd be better off without. Armed with freshly cut keys and a satchel of telephone equipment, we went up to the twelfth floor and attacked the alarm wires. As Bucky might have said, it was popcorn. Later, when I showed FBI men how easily Tommy and I had bypassed what they thought was a sophisticated system, they couldn't believe it. I had, with a telephone lineman's handset, a "toner," a cigar-sized probe and a couple of alligator clips, indentified the alarm wires for the door, bypassed the current and gotten past what they thought was an impregnable system. We were in.

Once in the treasury area we had only a thick slab of carbide steel between us and millions of dollars. The vault was double-doored, with combination locks on each side and an alarm. We poked around the room for a while and, *voilà*, found the combinations in a teller's drawer and the release switch for the alarm next to one of the tellers' windows. Taking note of the exact numbers the combination knobs were resting at, we released the locks—only to find what Bucky had suspected, that the big wheel that secured the doors was itself secured by a time lock. We had our work cut out for us.

While Bucky examined the vault, I continued rooting through the drawers and soon found some literature on the vault. Without even looking at it, I pocketed it quickly, saying nothing. I wanted to be able to look at it myself first. I wanted an edge on the others. We left, making sure everything was exactly as we found it. Outside we talked about the problem.

"Basically," Bucky said, "we got two options. One is burning rods, like we considered before. Problem is, with a vault like that you'd have to burn for a long time, and there'd be one hell of a lot of smoke. We'd have to punch a hole in the wall somewhere and funnel the smoke outside. Second option is better—I know with safes like these there's one spot that isn't carbide which you can drill through to and disconnect the time lock in case of an emergency. Too bad Charley ain't around, he'd know where."

"I know a safe guy," Joe said.

"OK. What you do is, next time we're in there you take pictures. The guy will know from them where to drill."

A week later we were back inside, Joe taking pictures and Bucky checking out the walls for a good spot to drill our funnel hole. But in the meantime I had read the literature on the vault and discovered that the time lock was set to a seventy-two hour schedule. On a four-day weekend like Thanksgiving I could come in here on the Sunday and rob the place by myself! But I said nothing.

The more I thought about it, the more I realized that the job was getting out of hand. Either of Bucky's options had serious drawbacks—both would require a lot of tools, which meant greater danger. Now that Joe's safe man knew about it he would have to be given a cut as well. But the biggest obstacle, the reason I primarily did not share my information about the time lock with the others, was the fact that I still had not seen a penny from Bucky. And as the months of planning went by, other evidence appeared that led me to believe that Bucky and probably Joe were spending a lot of money, money that could only have come from the stash.

Joe and Bucky traveled frequently to Las Vegas, and over one weekend lost $190,000. Joe and Brother put $50,000 down on a bar in Brighton, though they ended up reneging on the deal. Towards the end of 1981 Joe, Bucky and Bucky's pal Jake Rooney bought a bar on Broad Street in Boston called Angie's. They changed the name to the Little Rascals and did a roaring trade. When I confronted Joe about it he swore up and down that his share of the investment was only twenty-five grand. But I was suspicious.

I decided to do something about it. On a night I knew Bucky would be there I went to the Little Rascals and told him I had to talk. In my left pocket was a standard issue .357 magnum, loaded. If nothing else could convince Bucky of my concern, that would. He led me into the basement of the bar and closed the door behind him.

"What can I do for you, Jerry?"

"I want my fucking end, Bucky, and I want it now."

"Listen. I know you've—"

I pulled out the gun and stuck it in his face.

"I said I want my fucking end now."

Bucky went white. I thought he was going to shit his pants.

"Take it easy, Jerry."

"Don't tell me to take it easy. I'm tired of all this. I'm tired of being the guy who tells everybody else to calm down. I'm thinking maybe I've been a nice guy a little too long."

"Put the gun down. Please."

"The others wanted to take you out, you know that?"

"C'mon..."

"They wanted to finish you off, and now I'm thinking maybe I should have let them."

"Jerry, we can talk about this."

"So talk."

I lowered the gun. Bucky hitched at his lapels with shaking hands.

"I'm not going to lie to you. I haven't been able to move the stuff as quickly as I thought."

"Don't bullshit me, Bucky."

"No bullshit. Listen, you can have my end of the treasury job, OK? I swear to God."

I thought he was going to start blubbering any minute. He looked like a nervous child.

"Your end, your whole fucking end?"

From information we had rifled from the tellers' drawers, we knew there was over $3 million in the vault, so Bucky knew he was talking about at least $600,000, which would make my take $1.2 million. Compared to the four million or so in gold and jewelry I was expecting, that may not have seemed like much, but I'll take cash in the pocket over promised treasures any day.

"Absolutely."

"Another thing. I want some jewelry. Never mind moving it, I just want some jewels. I'll tell you how much I get for it."

"I'll get them to you next week."

I left with the information I wanted, feeling confident that I had convinced him of my anger and I fully expected to see some more money soon. But I was not prepared for what happened. The next time we all met to discuss the treasury job, Bucky announced, as if it were the only option we had left, that we'd have to bring in more people.

"What for?"

"Look, we need some safe people, people who know how these things operate. If we come in here, torch it up and get nothing, we get zilch dough and still gotta take the heat. Plus we need people to carry tools, to drive the truck. I know some guys, four guys, who we can count on to know what the fuck they're doing."

"Like who?"

"Sarducci and a few of his friends."

"I thought you said Sarducci liked to blow people's legs off for fun."

"We can count on him. He's a friend of mine."

Now I saw the writing on the wall. Bucky could see how serious I was about the stash and he wanted to cover his ass. He knew I knew he was screwing us, and he was scared. I wondered how I ever thought Bucky would part with a cool half million and decided to cut my losses. So I waited a couple of days and called the whole thing off, making excuses about security and police. The others could do nothing; after all, I was their in. I knew damn well that if I went in there with Bucky and his boys, I'd never come out alive. With my knowledge of the time lock and access to the building, I could have done the job myself, of course, but that too would have been enough to get me killed. And even a million bucks isn't much use to you when you're dead.

I called off the job in January 1982, when I was smack in the middle of my problems with the Metropolitan Police. Soon afterwards Joe delivered a small, plastic-wrapped package of jewels to me from Bucky. Now, I thought, we're getting somewhere. I carefully taped the package inside the wheel well of an old station wagon that my friend Dick Madden was going to drive down to Florida for me. I did not tell him it was there. I flew down to my condo in February and after a few weeks I brought the goods to a jeweler I knew there. Two days later I went back.

"Junk, Jerry, pure junk."

"What are you talking about?"

"It *was* good—at some point. But an expert's picked this clean. There's nothing here."

"You sure about this?"

"Positive."

I was fuming. Back at my condo I called Joe. No answer. I called Tommy and started yelling at him about Bucky. Tommy waited until I had vented my spleen and then calmly dropped a bombshell.

"Bucky's disappeared."

"Disappeared?"

"Yeah. He got busted a couple weeks ago in Southie. He had a warehouse full of marijuana there and somehow the DEA found out about it. When they moved in, Bucky got caught with pie all over his face. Jake Rooney was involved and Joe was supposed to be in on the deal, so he was bullshit when he heard what happened. But he's fucking lucky if you ask me. Bucky got out on bail and the next thing I heard he had disappeared."

"Did he jump?"

"That's what everybody thought at first, but word out on the street says otherwise."

"You think somebody took him out?" I asked.

"Let's put it this way," Tommy said. "I think we can forget about getting our shares from him."

So, I had nothing left but my suspicions, and my suspicions pointed directly at Joe Bangs. The more I thought about it, the more certain I was that he and Bucky had been dipping into the stash. He was a manipulator himself. I know now that while he was going into business with Bucky (legal and otherwise) he was arranging meetings that allowed me to get my anger out of my system and also gave me the false impression that Bucky was actually doing something about my share.

As I flew back to Boston that spring I resigned myself to having to deal with Joe Bangs, a man who at one time I thought of as my friend, but a man who was giving me more and more reason not to trust him. He was my last chance at getting any of the stash. But any chance that I may have had disappeared completely when I discovered Joe's latest venture. He was now moving into an area that would ultimately bring us all down. He was now moving into cocaine—and dragging Tommy with him.

8

Up in Smoke

I was a police officer for nearly twenty-five years, and during that time I participated in many activities that were not exactly legal. Somewhere along the line I lost sight of my purpose and role as a cop and my basic sense of right and wrong—and when greed blinded me, the opportunities for corruption were all too easily available. I've already talked about how my gradual slide into crime took place over those years and how completely I ended up submerged in corruption. I'm certainly not proud of that history. But to this day I can still claim that I managed to steer totally clear of one of the worst activities that anyone can involve himself in, the activity that turned our tight little gang into a self-destructive, disintegrating circle of scared men and unraveled our perfect crime—drugs.

Only someone living on a desert island for the last twenty years would not be aware of how extensive drug abuse has become in the United States since the 1960s. When I joined the Metropolitan Police in 1963, drugs were so uncommon that they were scarcely mentioned in my training. I can't remember making one drug bust over the course of my first five years there. But within a decade, what had been confined to a small subculture had expanded into the mainstream of American life. Drugs touched every corner of society, from junior high school corridors to corporate boardrooms. Today, most of us don't have to think too hard to picture someone we know whose life has been messed up by narcotics. And police officers are no exception.

Funnily enough, most people seem to view cops as being somehow removed from the drug culture. Even though your average policeman has more exposure to narcotics in one year than most people have in a lifetime, the public still seems to reason that, because police are responsible for battling drug use, collaring pushers and getting dope off the streets, they won't fall prey to the vice themselves. And the police, of course, give you the impression that this perception is true. But the facts say otherwise. Those who know cops well know the stories. Get past the silent brotherhood and a whole new world opens up, a world that almost every cop is aware of, even if he doesn't participate in it. When you combine the high rate of corruption with cops' constant contact with the problem, you end up with a significant number of police who regularly use drugs, and a hard-core group that keep its colleagues supplied.

Look at the papers. In the last couple of years there have been countless exposés exploring the problem—cops refusing to take urine tests, large quantities of heroin and cocaine disappearing from evidence rooms, cops taking bribes in the form of drugs. When you consider that for every discovered deceit there are probably dozens undetected, you begin to get some idea of the scope of the problem. I don't know of one police department that isn't tainted by drugs to some degree, and I couldn't count the number of cops I know who went on medical leave for "hypertension" or "nervous breakdowns," when actually they were spending time in drug rehab units kicking habits. The public rarely hears of police drug use because the police code forbids discussion outside the small brotherhood of cops, but it is there, believe me. Why do you think the police are so opposed to drug testing? There is a lot of talk about violation of civil rights and invasion of privacy, but beneath the talk and excuses is fear—fear that the public will discover the vast extent to which cops are hooked on coke, heroin, barbiturates, alcohol and speed. And as long as the unions and the brass pretend the problem doesn't exist, the longer it will be before the problem is solved. It will only get worse; drug use will only increase. The silence has to be broken, and what better way to break it than to make regular drug testing standard practice? Every recruit should be tested when he comes in, and every cop should be tested at least once a year. I'm convinced it is the only way to solve the problem.

Police drug abuse, like other kinds of police corruption, has implications that go well beyond the crime itself. When the men and women who are supposed to be eliminating drug use are using drugs themselves, then not only do they destroy themselves, they make sure that the problem is perpetuated. We don't have enough watchdogs to guard the watchdogs. And police salaries are hardly good enough to support chronic habits, so hooked cops frequently turn to petty crime, using their position to break into small businesses, pharmacies and private homes. Corruption breeds corruption, as my own career in crime illustrates. The possibilities for graft are endless.

Imagine this: Working an undercover drug operation, you burst in on a couple of big-time pushers who have a kilo of coke and ten grand in small bills sitting pretty on their kitchen table. You give your partner a knowing nod as you shake down the spread-eagled dealers, and before you can say Frank Serpico he has the cash and snow neatly tucked in his inside pockets. As you head out the door you tell the wide-eyed traffickers to screw. They don't know whether to be thankful they're not busted or angry you've stolen half their income for that month, but one thing's certain—they're sure as hell not going to rat on you. In the meantime you and your partner have, in five minutes, just earned the equivalent of two months' salary, tax-free. More significantly, you have thirty-seven ounces of coke, with a street value of two grand an ounce, sitting in the trunk of your cruiser. Fencing it at 100-percent profit to the users in your department will keep you in clover for a while, or the stuff may keep you flying high for a long time. Whatever way you look at it, you find it difficult to understand how you ever kept to the straight and narrow. You're making big money, keeping your buddies happy and not hurting anyone (or so you think). What more could you want?

If this scenario sounds like something out of a far-fetched novel, don't be fooled; it happens all the time and it happens in every major city in the United States. And the numbers in this example are modest. I knew a fellow cop who worked on an undercover drug unit for less than two years and got out because he was making too much money.

"I was bound to get caught, Jerry," he told me over a quiet beer one evening. "You wouldn't believe it. One time we went in one place and came out with fifty grand—fifty fucking grand in one day, can you believe it? The cash was fucking rolling in so fast I couldn't get rid of it. I bought a house down the Cape, a condo in Florida, a Cadillac, a swimming pool— and I still had dough left over. My partner was going over the edge, getting greedy. So I got out, Jerry, out like a bullet. I was scared. You know how it feels when it all seems too good to be true? You might think I'm crazy, but I asked for a transfer. It was only a matter of time before I got caught."

Now this guy was not what you would call a sleaze: he did not use drugs himself, he had kids and a wife to whom he remained faithful, and he owned an excellent record of public service. But the general attitude and the cancer of greed were too much for him—and before he knew it he was up to his ears. He was cool enough to get out, but the fact is he got to where he was in spite of his character—the system overtook him. And although he may have been clearing more than most, he was by no means exceptional.

Recently I was going into court with one of the biggest dealers in New England. He told me that cops regularly raided him for drugs and money only—no arrests. The odd thing was, he accepted it without surprise. Corruption was so common that he simply saw it as a business risk. I know from my own experience on the Metropolitan Police that a number of cops openly used and dealt, even on duty. Obviously they did what they could to conceal their activities from the brass, but among their peers cops made no effort to hide what they were doing.

I had plenty of experience of this myself. Because I was so scrupulous about keeping away from drugs completely, I was in a good position to see the damage they created. I saw lives destroyed. I saw the public put at risk because of the actions of police officers who were high while performing their duties, both within my own department and on other police forces. There was one lieutenant on the Medford PD who got so screwed up on coke that he saw enemies everywhere, even among his own friends. Tommy, who supplied him, told me that this guy would regularly appear on Tommy's driveway in the middle of the night, yelling at the top of his lungs that Tommy was stealing his girlfriend, a woman Tommy hardly even knew.

One time I was down at the Medford station, shooting the breeze with Tommy, when a young guy with shoulder-length hair was brought in under arrest. The charge was minor, and the guy looked relatively harmless. Behind the desk was another screwed-up cop, a guy I knew was a heavy user, and that night I could see from his jittery, hard-edged behavior that he was high right there on the job. When the arrested man came before him, the cop leaned over the desk, wild-eyed and hyper, and shouted:

"What's your name?"

The guy took a step to the left and said nothing.

"I said, what's your name?"

No reply. The cop picked up a pair of scissors, reached across, grabbed the guy's hair and cut off a lock.

"Hey, what the hell are you doing?"

"Tell me your fucking name!"

"No way."

He cut off more hair. Looking around the room, I saw that the other cops were tense and alert.

"All right," the guy shouted, "all right..."

He yelled out his name and the cop put the scissors away. The cop did nothing else, but the incident made me uneasy. There was something uncontrolled, something violent in that cop's eyes. It wasn't long before I would see that kind of latent violence appearing in Tommy and Joe.

If ordinary, reputable guys like my friend in the undercover drug unit were involved so heavily, imagine what a real hood like Joe Bangs was doing. It was some time after the Depositors Trust heist before I discovered the extent of Joe's involvement with drugs, but when I did it blew me away. He got in so fast and so deep that I couldn't believe it. He and Bucky used the proceeds of the robbery—including money from the jewelry that should have been split between us—to purchase huge amounts of marijuana and cocaine for distribution throughout New England. Joe was a middleman between organized crime and local dealers, and he dealt in huge amounts; on at least one occasion he oversaw the sale of two truckloads of marijuana, about ten thousand pounds. Millions of dollars passed through his hands, and his own profits must have been very generous. He was certainly living the high life, jetting to Vegas and the Bahamas and gambling away hundreds of thousands of dollars. He wasn't doing all that on a Metropolitan policeman's salary. He took advantage of Bucky's contacts and he created a lot of his own. And he was smart. Joe had a nose for a bad deal and an unerring sense of who was safe to deal with. If a fed or a rat was on board, Joe always seemed to know and left the ship before it was too late. He had brains and luck, and he made a lot of dough.

But as much as Joe was making from marijuana, his profits skyrocketed when he got into coke. By the time Bucky disappeared in late 1982, Joe had already established a reputation as a major dealer. Soon he was clearing fifteen grand a week, *profit*. On the Metropolitan Police he developed a reputation as a supplier for hooked cops, and by 1983 the brass were conducting an internal investigation of his affairs. As much as that robbery gold must have been worth to him, coke was his real tender now. Drugs were his livelihood, and being a policeman was useful primarily for establishing contacts and avoiding the law. He had a large crew of associates to do his bidding, including one cop who sold snow from the saddlebags of his motorcycle.

A hard core of Metropolitan cops did serious drugs, and they were frequent guests at Joe's infamous parties in the Boston suburb of Everett, where hookers, booze and a variety of narcotics were always in plentiful supply. When I heard of these parties I used to wonder how the neighbors tolerated that kind of scene, but as Joe said to me once, who's going to call cops on cops? Actually, the residents of the apartment complex felt secure knowing the cops were there, even if the goings-on were somewhat bizarre. And Joe's clientele wasn't just from the Metropolitan force; cops from Medford, Somerville, Boston and other local towns were regulars.

My attitude towards this whole scene was one of extreme caution. Frankly, drugs scared me—not because they were illegal, but because I knew what they could do to people. Even though there was tremendous money to be made, it was my experience that anybody who got into the business could not help becoming a user himself. And once you are a user, you've lost your freedom, something which, as I sit in my jail cell here and think back on these events, I have come to appreciate a lot.

I never could understand the appeal of drugs. The thought of smoking a joint or snorting coke has always been offensive to me. I've never smoked a cigarette in my life, and I don't even take aspirin unless it is absolutely necessary. Even the FBI agents who were on my trail for years told me after my apprehension that they were amazed I had never gone anywhere near narcotics. Everyone else in our gang had. Bucky and Kenny were into some heavy dealing. Joe, of course, learned the trade very quickly, and he kept Brother supplied. That left Tommy, the last person you would expect to become a heavy user. But somewhere along the line even Tommy must have wondered what was so great about this stuff, and he too went under. Only I kept my head above water. I kept clear of the whole mess because I saw what drugs did to people and I didn't want it to happen to me. Guys who were friendly and level-headed changed completely. They were never themselves. I saw cops who, in a matter of months, would leave their families, move in with a hooker and spend every spare minute high on cocaine. They stopped communicating; they stopped being real people. The way I looked at it, life was tough enough to handle when I was straight—hooked on a poison that wouldn't allow me to think was the last thing in the world I needed, especially when my own wits were the sole thing between keeping my freedom and going to jail. Unfortunately I had no control over the wits of Tommy and Joe.

I had plenty of evidence that Joe was getting more and more screwed up. He talked a lot about taking people out. He waved his gun around with abandon. When I broke up with Barbara Hickey, I would often express to him my worry that she would (as she eventually did) do something drastic to get back at me. For a while I had been monitoring her telephone and watching her house. She had frequent contact with some guys I didn't know, and I was worried they were the feds. I attached a simple listening device to the telephone wires outside her house, which I could monitor from my car radio. Tommy and I would park in the lot of a nearby sandwich shop and listen. Once or twice she would be visited by men I didn't know, and Tommy and I would follow them. But we came up with nothing. After quite a few sessions during which I heard nothing to suggest she was cooperating with the law, I gave that up. But I was still worried. Joe had a simple solution.

"Do you want me to kill her?" he asked.

"Are you nuts?"

"Listen, I'll burn her fucking house down, I know exactly how to do it. I get a couple gallons of gas in a plastic jug and set a hair dryer so that it's blowing on the jug. I take off, the jug heats up, and kablooie."

"I'm not interested, Joe."

"Hey, just offering."

The guy was getting dangerous. Ironically, after all the shit he went through and put me through, Joe testified to this conversation in my trial, but he reversed the roles, saying that I asked him to kill her or burn down her house. But by then he was lying about everything.

It didn't really surprise me to discover that Tommy and Joe went into the drug business together. Tommy had money to invest and connections to exploit that Joe could certainly profit from. And for his part, Tommy looked on with increasing envy as Joe's life got glitzier and glitzier. Joe was strutting around town with a hooker on each arm and custom-made diamond rings on his fingers. He had Cadillacs in his driveway and a new swimming pool in his back yard. He threw money around as if it were water and never allowed you to go for your wallet. Tommy was impressed. Tommy had never been a flamboyant guy, he had never tried to impress people with wealth, but as he joined Joe in the world of drug-dealing he began to change, trying to play the part of the high roller. He always was a hustler. He was continually looking to score extra cash when he could, so no doubt he saw a golden opportunity here to invest some of his share in Joe's lucrative enterprise.

So Tommy and Joe started doing business. Joe would supply Tommy, who would supply local cops and small dealers. At first he was reasonably discreet, but with his connections on the Medford PD, soon Tommy was dealing blatantly from his barn on Pleasant Street and his tool rental business downtown. It became common knowledge that, in Medford, Tommy was the one to see for coke. He prospered.

But gradually I started to notice changes in his behavior. He became distant. He brought hookers back to his barn, even though his wife was sitting in the house across the street. He worked less and less on his houses and spent more of his time cooped up indoors. And he started trying to dress like a big-shot, which really should have told me Tommy was changing. Tommy had always been a casual guy—he wore work pants and flannel shirts and heavy boots whenever he was out of uniform. Now he was trying to dress like Joe, and it just wasn't Tommy.

But I still didn't suspect he was using until July 1983, when Tommy, a girlfriend of his and I were staying at my condo in Florida. Joe and his girlfriend were also in town, and one afternoon Joe was over at my place having a beer. I went into the kitchen to get a bottle opener, and when I returned Joe and Tommy had gone into Tommy's bedroom. I walked in on them as they were snorting coke out of a little bottle with a nose-pipe. Joe looked up at me with a smile.

"Hey, Jerry, want a blast?"

I said nothing, but I was shocked. Here it was, a beautiful, hot afternoon in July, and Tommy and Joe were snorting poison. I felt that, somehow, I had been betrayed, that my own apartment had been dirtied. It wasn't that they had hidden their use from me; I was simply scared that they would change.

After that incident they no longer kept their use a secret, and soon I saw that both of them were into it pretty heavily. I insisted they keep the stuff away from me. Joe, I knew, was probably a lost cause, but Tommy I worked on. Why are you doing this shit? I kept asking him. Don't you realize what you're getting into? I can handle it, he insisted, over and over again, I can handle it. But the evidence suggested otherwise to me.

Tommy was my friend, so naturally I was worried. But my fears ran deeper. We were all in a race together—the five of us (Bucky had disappeared by now) against the FBI, the state police, the D.A. and anyone else trying to prove what we had done and get us behind bars. The finishing tape was the statute of limitations—five years according to federal law and six according to state law. May 31, 1986, we would all be home free, forever. And I was certain that by now they could never nail us unless one of us made a big mistake—and drugs, I knew, could make people do some very strange things. If Joe and Tommy got into a situation where one burned the other—a very likely situation, it seemed to me—then the temptation for the other to strike back by testifying about their drug connections and the bank job would be extreme. And I could go down with them.

It was only a matter of time before Joe and Tommy started freebasing. There is a law of diminishing returns in drug use:the more you use, the weaker the effect, and the greater the concentration you look for. And nothing concentrates coke like freebasing. The first time I saw Tommy do it I was amazed at how much coke he had to use for one hit, but by then he and Joe were dealing in such large amounts that they had plenty to burn. They weren't dealing in ounces, or even in pounds. Coke was passing through their hands by the kilo, and I knew of at least one deal where five kilos were involved. When Tommy freebased, he would mix a large amount of coke with water and baking soda and put this mixture over direct flame or in a pot of boiling water. When the mixture turned to an oily liquid, he removed it, cooling it rapidly with cold water. The liquid hardened, and Tommy broke off pieces of it, called "rocks," and smoked them in a pipe.

Freebasing completed the change in Tommy. He stopped working altogether—he left the Medford force on sick time and didn't bother working on his houses at all. He had contractors doing work on his property whom he paid with coke. He would spend all day in the barn/office he owned across the street from his house, smoking every fifteen minutes and sleeping half the day. He had two cats in there who were always knocked out because of the smoke, and whenever I visited him there was a blue haze hanging over his money-covered desk. A steady stream of clients flowed up Pleasant Street to his barn. I was building a garage at the time, so I was going up there quite often to borrow tools or lumber. Whenever I had the opportunity, I would talk to Tommy about his situation. I never got anywhere. There were times when I'd stay away for a while and Tommy would call me up.

"Where the fuck have you been?"

"What do you mean?" I said.

"You avoiding me or what? I haven't seen you up here in a long time."

"I'm surprised you noticed."

"What's that supposed to mean?"

"You're coked up all the time, Tommy, you're in a fucking haze. I don't want to be around when they finally hit your place."

"Who's going to hit me, answer me that?"

"One of these kids you've been supplying is gonna get busted, Tommy, and then you're going down the fucking tubes. I was talking to your partner," I said, mentioning the name of Tommy's associate in the tool rental business, "and he's bullshit. He says you're dealing out of the store for Christ's sake. I mean, is that stuff cooking your brain cells? You're doing stupid things, Tommy, you know that, don't you?"

"I can handle it."

"I never see you working anymore. I never see you around town. And you're asking me where *I've* been?"

"I can handle it, Jerry."

Nothing I said impressed him; I was up against too seductive an enemy. What I had seen happening to so many others was now happening to Tommy right before my eyes, and there was nothing I could do about it.

Soon Tommy and Joe widened the scope of their activities, clinching big deals all over the country and using their contacts to widen the net of their customers and increase their profits. The amounts—of drugs and money—got larger, and the stakes got higher. An aura of violence began to surround their dealings. The aura suited Joe—he had always collided with the world in his own belligerent way—but not Tommy. He had never been an overtly violent guy. He had never been threatening, even though he knew how to take care of himself. Drugs were really beginning to skew his vision of the world, and I did my best to steer clear.

Joe had cops going to Florida for him, strapping huge amounts of coke to their bodies and flying back. He had developed underworld sources who wanted to take advantage of his police connections, and slowly he became the big-time hood he had always dreamed of being. Tommy had his own cadre of conspirators who operated out of the barn in Medford. Two of the biggest were Al Roberts, an ex-Medford cop, and Jackie Gillen, the brother-in-law whom Tommy had lost his job for back in 1972. Jackie bought huge amounts of coke from Tommy and his pals, cut it severely, and sold it throughout South Boston. And he was not exactly discreet. Jackie was known for his loose lips and his failure to attend to detail—dangerous qualities in a man who made his living from crime.

All sorts of minor figures got involved in the drama, so many that I couldn't keep track of them. One day I went over to Tommy's barn and let myself in. A Medford cop, someone I knew was a heavy user and a runner for Tommy, was bent over the desk, scraping the top with a razor blade. He was so desperate for coke that he was busting his balls trying to scrape the residue of Tommy's deals into a tiny plastic bag. He was in uniform. Later I found out that that same guy was breaking into businesses in Medford, on duty, to support his habit. Tommy had a whole crew of associates like him, all protected by a corrupt police brotherhood.

But given the kind of guys surrounding him and the amount of coke he was pumping into his system, it was only a matter of time before things fell apart. The summer of 1983 was a turning point, though it would be a while before that was fully apparent. In August Gillen finally made the big gaffe that he was destined to make. He had arranged for a consignment of twenty-five tons of marijuana to be delivered to a port near Portland, Maine, from a Haitian ship. But when he boarded,

the feds nailed him. There was a rat right in the group of guys
Gillen was dealing with, a guy from the DEA, and the gang
had been tailed and watched the whole way. Tommy had lent
Jackie some guns and a police radio. I remember seeing him
and Joe the night of the deal, talking about Gillen and waiting
for the ship to come in. When they heard the news, Tommy
was worried about the radio, but he knew that no one could
conclusively prove his involvement. He was relieved he wasn't
caught red-handed. Joe, however, was bullshit. For a while
now he had been angry about Gillen's loose dealings and Tommy's indiscretion. One night the following week I saw him
with Brother at the Embassy Lounge in Somerville. In a loud
voice he complained about Tommy and his cohorts for ten
minutes. He gesticulated wildly and stared at me with coked-
out eyes.

"I hope they lock Gillen up," he concluded, "and throw
away the fucking key. Everything he touches turns to shit.
And Roberts—that asshole shouldn't be selling joints on
Boston Common. What's with Tommy and these guys? Does
he have his head up his ass or what?"

Before I had a chance to answer he was chasing some hooker
out the door. I turned to Brother, who was sitting there with
raised eyebrows, high on coke himself.

"He been like this for long?" I asked.

Brother nodded.

"The guy is unbelievable," he said. "He's smoking rocks
the size of quarters every half hour. I mean, that would kill
anybody besides him."

"How long does this go on?"

"Three, four days. He hasn't been to sleep for seventy-two
hours, and look at him, he's still hyper. I tell you one thing,
though—you don't want to be around when he crashes. He's
got a violent streak in him that isn't very pretty."

"How does he manage to do business?"

"He manages better than Tommy does. What's Tommy's
problem, anyway?"

"The problem is," I said, "that Tommy can't take the stuff like Joe can. The stuff is frying his brains and he doesn't even know it."

But whether he knew it or not, he continued working with Joe and trying to match his lifestyle. Together they bought a condo in Pompano Beach, Florida, for eighty-two grand (though Joe was a silent partner) and spent a lot of time jetting back and forth between there and Boston. Tommy branched out, doing major deals on his own, but he kept working with Joe through the winter of '83-84. But it wasn't long before that world started to disintegrate.

By then Joe and Tommy were freebasing exclusively. Tommy was in outer space most of the time. One day I went over to his barn, walked right in and saw him slumped over in his chair. I thought he was dead, but he was fast asleep, like his two cats. Stacks of twenties covered the whole desk—not one square inch of the desktop was visible. Anyone could have waltzed in and walked away with a small fortune, because it took me five minutes to shake him awake.

For his part, Joe was roaring around town in his Cadillac, doing deals and being seen in the right places. After retiring from the Metropolitan Police on disability for hypertension in February 1984, he spent a lot of time in Boston's Logan Airport, flying regularly to Vegas and Atlantic City for gambling binges and junketing to Canada, the Midwest, Florida and the Bahamas in pursuit of drugs. He traveled under a variety of aliases. He had tens of thousands of dollars rolling around in the trunks of his cars, more money than he seemed to know what to do with. He kept smoking his rocks and chasing his hookers, and it didn't look like much was going to change. He had left his wife and now lived across the street from Tommy's barn, renting a house from Tommy.

Then Joe fell in love. In April 1984 he started seeing a woman named Debbie O'Malley, a good-looking blonde with two kids, a taste for coke and an ability to match Joe's high lifestyle. Joe tumbled for her in a big way, and soon she was his constant companion. But Joe was not the kind of guy to say it with flowers. With his personality, you could be sure that Joe's reaction to falling in love would be negative. He became insanely possessive and jealous, and every man became a potential threat. Fueled by his addiction, he would get into huge arguments with her, slapping her around and grilling her about past lovers. He would abuse her to the point where she would finally scream at him the worst possible thing he could hear—that such-and-such a guy they both knew was better in the sack than Joe. Her remarks would really send him over the edge, and after giving her a couple extra blows for good measure he would go down to the unsuspecting guy's house and pistol-whip him as he shouted incoherent accusations. He had a strange way of expressing his affection.

But Bangs's jealousy was to get even more absurd, to the point where he was imagining liaisons and seeing rivals in even his best friends. He was often seen dragging a screaming O'Malley from his car by her hair while kids played on the sidewalks of Pleasant Street. She accompanied him on a number of his Vegas trips, trips that usually ended in huge, cocaine-induced fights during which Joe would smash hotel furniture and threaten to kill her. After one particularly nasty trip in August of 1984 she returned to Boston alone. Joe called Tommy from Vegas and warned him not to pick her up. He was suspicious even of Tommy, who was probably his closest pal. "This is my affair," he told him, "and I want you to stay out of it." But Tommy picked her up anyway— he didn't see any harm in it—and Joe's displeasure thickened with paranoia and animosity.

Tommy was doing so much coke himself, he too became psychotic. And to make matters worse, Tommy's money problems deepened. His financial sense had drifted away in a cloud of cocaine smoke, and his debts were extensive, particularly to Joe. Joe, who you would think must have been spending more than anyone could possibly make, managed to keep his head above water. For some reason—street smarts or some kind of sixth sense or plain blind luck—Joe always managed to steer clear of bad deals. Tommy, on the other hand, was on a crash course—with the law, with his connections and with Joe.

In August a former Medford cop named Mickey Burns introduced Tommy to an ex-prisonmate of his, a guy who claimed he could arrange a $45,000 coke deal down in Tennessee. Without properly investigating the people involved, Tommy committed himself. He asked Joe to go with him, but he refused. He smelled something wrong with the deal and he didn't like the way Tommy was arranging things. Nor was he too fond of Al Roberts, whom Tommy was bringing to Nashville. Roberts had lived with Debbie O'Malley before she met Joe, so naturally Joe thought he was still after her. Joe did lend Tommy ten grand, however, and after borrowing heavily from other sources, Tommy headed south in his brand-new Lincoln with Roberts and Burns. There must have been some miscommunication about money, because a day or two later Tommy sent Burns back to Boston with a request for another fourteen grand from Bangs. Joe handed over another thirteen, pretending it was in fact fourteen.

The deal went sour, and Tommy and Roberts drove to Boston $60,000 poorer. But they only stayed long enough to arm themselves with sawed-off shotguns, and they returned south to retaliate. After unsuccessfully scouring the Nashville area for the guy, they started looking for another deal. Tommy was desperate—he was in debt up to his ass and he had just blown sixty grand, none of which was his own. Coked up every minute, he did not act rationally and indiscreetly spread the word that he was looking to deal, even though he had no money. He got his deal, or so he thought, in Jackson, Mississippi. Tommy met a guy in a hotel lounge who said he could set him up with a couple kilos, and they arranged a meet on a nearby golf course. I don't know what he did about money, but Tommy sent Roberts to the course in the Lincoln. As soon as Roberts opened the trunk to receive the coke, he was busted. They got Tommy a few minutes later, and he tried to claim he was on a sting operation that the undercover cops had ruined. They didn't buy it. I found this out from Joe, whom I met outside Tommy's house the next day. It was the first time I had seen him in nearly a year, and I was shocked at his pale, puffy face. He was fuming.

"That fucking asshole," he said of Doherty, "I knew he was screwing up, I knew I should never have given him that dough."

He kicked the door of the barn. His hands were shaking and his pupils dilated.

"If he'd listened to me," Joe said, "he wouldn't have got into this fucking mess in the first place. That son of a bitch lied to me, lied to my face."

"What's wrong?"

He told me about the bust.

"And the feds are involved since they crossed state lines with weapons. This time he's going away, you know that, don't you? I'll never see that fucking money again. I'm moving out of here. I'm not having anything to do with that asshole again. One of these days, Jerry, he's going to take us all down with him."

I'd heard enough of Joe's harangues, so I made an excuse and left. I could see that my efforts to keep Tommy on a safe path were failing, and my mind was busy with strategies to keep his indiscretions contained. As long as I could keep him and Joe at arm's length from each other, I felt we had a fighting chance of making it to the statute of limitations, which was still over a year and a half away. But I would never have predicted what would happen that October, sending all my efforts of reconciliation into the toilet.

The tension level that month was incredibly high. Tommy and Roberts, who had posted bail in Mississippi after the bust and pleaded not guilty, were indicted. Gillen went on trial for the Maine fiasco and Joe was reaching a fever-pitch in his love-hate relationship with Debbie. One night Bangs, O'Malley and

Tommy were freebasing in Tommy's barn while Joe bugged Tommy about money. When he saw he wasn't getting anywhere with Tommy, he turned on O'Malley, making his usual accusations. Something inside him snapped, and he grabbed her, shaking her violently and waving a .357 magnum under her nose. Tommy grabbed Joe's wrist and, after a brief tussle, wrestled the gun away.

"Listen," he yelled at Joe, "you pull this shit one more time, you pull this gun out in my house, and I'll shove it up your ass."

Joe backed off and dragged Debbie from the house. It was very unlike Tommy to challenge Joe like that. Things were coming to a head.

On the morning of October 16 I had coffee at Tommy's barn. He seemed a little jumpier than usual, but I had stopped trying to predict his moods for some time. He talked a little about the Mississippi case and then lowered his voice.

"Listen Jerry, I got to tell you something. I don't know if you noticed, but Joe's going off the deep end fast."

"I heard about him and that hooker, if that's what you mean."

"It's more than that. He's been pistol-whipping people all over the goddam place, and for no good reason. That card-dealer in Boston," he mentioned the guy's name, "he got really pissed. And he's not the only one."

"So what are you saying?"

"Well, between you and me—you know Guido, the jeweler? He told me that something was going to be done about it. I told him, listen, just don't do it in my place, you know what I mean?"

"What, someone's going to take Joe out?"

"Hey, it isn't like he isn't asking for it. He doesn't give a shit who he pushes around anymore."

By this stage I wasn't overly fond of Joe, but the news disturbed me. I stood up.

"People talk like that all the time, Tommy. It doesn't mean nothing."

He shrugged.

"Look," I said, "I'll drop by later. I need some lumber."

"Don't bother. I'm having a guest up here."

He smiled. I was getting tired of him and his hookers.

"Whatever turns you on, Tommy."

"Whaddayasay you come by later tonight, midnight or so, and we'll have a beer."

"Sure."

I didn't know it then, but Tommy had planned the whole conversation. He was using me to establish an alibi.

I returned home to work on my garage. Around lunchtime I was downtown, where I ran into two Medford cops. They told me they had been outside Tommy's a half-hour earlier and seen Bangs dragging Debbie from one side of the street to the other, beating her up and pistol-whipping her. They couldn't believe their eyes, but they certainly were not going to step between them. Pleasant Street had become a little city within a city, exempt from law and reason and anything resembling normal behavior.

Mid-afternoon I returned to Tommy's for lumber and tools. I saw Jackie Gillen crossing the lawn, so I called him over.

"Tommy around?"

"He's around, all right, but he ain't gonna answer the door. He's got a hooker in there and he won't be out for a while."

He gestured towards the barn. I could see Tommy's wife's car in the driveway across the street. He had created a strange world for himself.

"No point in staying around here, Jerry. You're not going to see him today."

I got the impression Gillen wanted to get rid of me, but before I could answer, we heard a high-pitched squeal of rubber as Joe Bangs's Cadillac roared up, bouncing up and down as he drove up onto the sidewalk. A woman sat in the passenger seat. I could hear her yelling at Joe as he got out of the car and approached the door of the barn. When he found it locked he started kicking the door and swearing.

"Look at that asshole," Gillen said, "he's so coked up he doesn't even see us."

Gillen was right. Joe wasn't ten yards away and he acted as if he were alone. He went back to the car and started hitting the woman, belting her with such force that we could hear the blows from where we stood. Her screams echoed along the quiet street. I looked at Gillen uneasily.

"Is that O'Malley?" I had never seen her.

"Yeah."

Joe got out again and attacked the barn door with even more force. Now the woman got out of the car and ran down the street. Joe got back in his car and floored it, knocking over trash barrels as he spun a circle and took off after her. Gillen walked away, shaking his head. I felt peculiar, as if I had been watching a movie. I took a last look at the barn and went home.

About eleven-thirty, as I was considering joining Tommy for that beer he suggested, he called me.

"Hey Jerry, could we make that another time? There's cops all over the place down here chasing Gillen."

He was very calm and made the excuse as if he were saying his mother-in-law was coming over for dinner.

"What's wrong?"

"Oh, you know, Gillen and his usual shit. I'll talk to you tomorrow."

I went to bed. At three in the morning the phone interrupted my dreams, and Carmen Marullo's voice floated over the wire. Marullo was a Medford cop who also worked as an investigator for the flamboyant trial lawyer Thomas Troy.

"Bangs has been shot," he said. 'I thought you should know that."

"Is he all right?"

"I don't know. I thought I heard the ambulance men say he was dying."

"Who did it?"

"Who do you think?"

So Tommy had gone over the edge. I lay in the darkness and stared at the digital clock, thinking of what might happen if Joe survived. I got no more sleep that night.

9

Payback Is a Bitch

I didn't see any point in going over to Tommy's house right away. I didn't particularly want to be seen there by the authorities, and I was certain to be informed of the details soon. If Joe died I'd find out quick enough. I still couldn't believe that after trying to blow Joe away Tommy had calmly called me and canceled our meeting. Tommy always was a cool customer, but this time his calmness was unreal. Maybe the seriousness of his position hadn't yet reached his coked-out brain.

But Tommy wasn't the only one whose position was serious. The implications of the shooting affected me as well. If Joe survived, he had every reason to avenge himself, and what more satisfactory way to get back at Tommy than to turn him in for the bank? The problem was, of course, that if Joe were to get immunity for his own participation in the crime, he would have to tell the whole truth or risk losing that immunity. He couldn't go after Tommy selectively; Brother, Kenny and I would go too. Conversely, Tommy might now try to beat Joe to the punch. Anticipating Joe's revenge, he might go for immunity himself. Both possibilities kept me from sleep.

When I went over to Pleasant Street the following morning, the scene had still not quieted down. Fire engines, local police cruisers and state troopers filled the street in front of the house. Curious Medford residents milled about the area while television cameramen and reporters ran back and forth. I kept my distance, watching from behind my car at the end of the street. After a few minutes I heard a horn blowing, turned around and saw Brother waving me over from behind the wheel of his car.

"What do you think?" I said.

"I heard about it on TV. Couldn't believe my ears—didn't believe them until they showed the house. I started worrying right away. Do you know what this means? The whole fucking thing's going to come out now. If Tommy doesn't rat then Joe will."

"Not necessarily," I said.

"What, you don't think Joe won't want revenge?"

"He might not live to get revenge. I heard he's dying."

"I wouldn't count on it, not with Joe involved. That son of a bitch is so lucky..."

Brother nervously tapped the top of the steering wheel.

"You know, Jerry, I had a funny feeling it would come to this, a funny feeling."

"Why?"

"Oh shit," he said, "look who's coming."

I looked up and saw an agitated, thick-featured woman running towards us. Her blouse was bloodstained and her pupils were like saucers.

"O'Malley?"

"Yeah," Brother said.

It was the first time I had seen her face. As she approached the car she kept looking over her shoulder. She stuck her head in the driver's-side window.

"Brother, did you hear what happened?"

"Yeah."

"Those assholes have taken the keys to his Cadillac," she said. "They're going into his trunk."

She was talking ninety miles an hour, higher than a 747.

"Who?"

"Those fucking troopers," she said. "There's a kilo of coke in there, there's money, there's all kinds of shit, and they're going to find it."

The only person I had ever seen as hyper as O'Malley was acting was Joe. I saw now that, in her, Joe had found a partner, someone with the personality and habits to suit the point he'd reached in his life.

"How's Joe?" Brother asked.

"He got it with a shotgun, in the chest and the back. God, the blood..."

Her voice trailed away. Brother introduced me to her, but she seemed not to hear. She fluttered nervously at the window and put her hand on the roof.

"Brother, move over," she said.

"What for?"

"Let's do some lines."

I couldn't believe it. The man she was living with, the man that, presumably, she loved, was in the hospital, dying, a corps of police was a hundred feet away, and here she was suggesting to Brother that they snort coke right here in the car. That was enough for me—I jumped out, got into my car and drove home. I didn't need this shit, especially when I had a crisis on my hands.

That afternoon I sat at home and waited for the news. I figured that if Joe was OK he would try to get in touch with me. About three o'clock I got the call I was waiting for. Joe's cousin phoned and told me Joe was all right. He had some pretty severe wounds, but he was going to live. He wouldn't say any more over the phone but insisted I meet him outside St. Francis's Church in Medford within the hour.

"Joe wants to see you," he said at the church. "He says you're the only one who can keep this together."

"Where is he?"

"Lawrence Memorial Hospital in Medford. They worked on him all last night. They said if he hadn't been high on coke he would have died of shock. Can you get that? The lucky bastard lives because he's out of his fucking head."

But that was Joe. The guy had more lives than a cat and more luck than Houdini. I drove straight to the hospital, and when I went into his room he was out of bed, lurching back from the bathroom like an old man. He looked like hell—

after all, he had just been on a three-day coke binge and taken a couple blasts from a shotgun. He immediately started ranting about Tommy.

"That motherfucker," he screamed, "he tried to assassinate me. After all I've done for him that son of a bitch tried to take me out, and he couldn't even do it like a man."

"Calm down, Joe, calm down."

"He's a rat, Jerry, a sneaky rat with no guts. He couldn't even take the first shot himself, he had that asshole Gillen do it. You know something? I'll meet that motherfucker one-on-one in a field any day. Just me and him and a couple of guns. He wants a shootout? I'll give him a fucking shootout."

He coughed uncontrollably. I thought he was going to have a heart attack. Ashen-faced and droop-eyed, he trembled when he talked and moved his arm stiffly through the air. Beneath his loose hospital johnny I could see the thick bandages. He lay on his side and breathed fitfully as he spoke.

"He did this for money and coke. All I've done for him, our friendship—it means nothing. And what if he *had* killed me? He would have had to kill Debbie and her kid too, because they knew where I was. Can you believe that? I mean, it's one thing taking me out, but the woman and her sixteen-year-old girl? That guy doesn't have a manly bone in his fucking body."

"Listen Joe, just tell me what happened. *Slowly.*"

Between outbursts of spleen directed at Tommy, Joe told me the story. The previous night he had driven to the Memory Lane bar in Somerville, where he met a friend for a beer. He was driving a green Chevrolet that belonged to an old girlfriend, and in the trunk were a kilo of coke, some jewelry, $10,000 in Canadian money, airline tickets and a canvas gym bag containing two guns. Debbie O'Malley and her daughter Kelly joined him at the bar a half an hour later, and after one drink they left for a restaurant in South Boston, transferring the items from the trunk of the Chevy to the trunk of Joe's Cadillac, which Debbie had driven over from Pleasant Street.

After dinner, Joe, Debbie and her daughter returned to their house. After the daughter had gone to bed, Joe and Debbie freebased for a while. About ten-thirty, Tommy called Joe and told him he had some money for him. He also asked him to bring over some coke. Joe told him that he was getting ready to go out, and that he would be over in a while. About forty-five minutes later Joe called him, told him he was coming and then crossed the street to the barn, unarmed. He had some coke in his right-hand jacket pocket.

Tommy's barn was two stories high. The first floor was a two-car garage with bay doors and an average-sized metal door on the left. A spiral staircase led up to the second floor, where Tommy had his office. When Joe arrived at the barn, he found the metal door locked. He knocked, and Al Roberts, who was working on a car in the garage, let him in.

"Where are they?"

Roberts nodded at the staircase.

"Up there."

As Joe mounted the staircase he saw Roberts lock the door. At that point he thought nothing of it. When he got to the closed door of Tommy's office, he knocked and yelled, "Tommy, it's me, Joe." Tommy yelled for him to come in. When Joe opened the door he saw Jackie Gillen crouched in front of him, his teeth clenched, pointing a sawed-off twelve-gauge shotgun at Joe's chest. Tommy was hiding behind his desk. Joe heard a huge blast and thought he was dreaming. The shotgun pellets spun him around, but he felt no pain. He put his left hand to his chest and felt blood. As he ran towards the staircase he heard another peal of thunder, and pellets ripped into his back. He managed to reach the garage door quickly, but as Roberts had locked it Joe had to take his left hand from the wound and work the deadbolt back. His right arm was dead. As he worked at the bolt he turned around and saw Tommy standing on the staircase, pointing a long-barreled revolver at him. Tommy fired twice, missing both times. Joe finally opened the door and ran across the street.

He couldn't get his keys out of his pocket, so he kicked at the door of his house, yelling at Debbie that he had been shot. She opened the door and helped him upstairs.

"Get me a gun," he said. "Wake up Kelly and put her in the bathroom."

Debbie was scared to death. She left him draped over the couch and ran into her bedroom, where she grabbed his .38. Without consulting Joe she phoned an ambulance and the police.

"What the hell are you doing?" he yelled.

"Calling the cops."

"The cops, the fucking Medford cops? Are you out of your mind? Tommy's a fucking *Medford* cop."

He half-lay on the floor, propped up against the couch, the gun in his left hand, blood pouring from his wounds, and waited for the cops. He did not expect to live.

Now, Joe was not shot with a BB-gun. The automatic shot-gun that Gillen fired twice at close range sent nine pellets of double-O buck, pellets each the size of a .38 slug, *through* Joe's body. Not one of those pellets touched a bone, that was how lucky Joe was. Of course, the coke that he had just freebased had an anesthitizing effect, as his cousin told me, and protected Joe's system from shock, but whatever way you look at, Joe was one fortunate son of a bitch. Anybody else would have keeled over right there. And Joe's fortune was Tommy's downfall—and mine as well.

A nurse came in to dress Joe's wounds, and when I saw the condition of his chest I nearly got sick. He had a wound the size of a basketball and the color of congealed blood. I learned later that when the police arrived at Joe's house, one of them actually put his hand into his chest and pinched a severed artery, saving his life. Even as the nurse worked on him, Joe continued his tirade against Tommy, and I saw that I was going to have a lot of work to do to keep these two from bringing us all down the tubes.

Joe was in hospital for three weeks, a state trooper at the door of his room the entire time in case someone should come and try to finish the job. I visited him regularly, and I also kept in touch with Tommy. In fact, I lent Tommy five grand to bail himself out on the shooting charge. Though he was careful about what he told me, he also filled me in on the rest of the story.

When the police and ambulance crew arrived at Pleasant Street that night they found a quiet scene. Doherty, Gillen and Roberts were sipping coffee in Doherty's office. Thomas Troy, a former Metropolitan cop turned defense lawyer who would eventually defend Doherty in the trial for attempted murder, had already joined them. Outside, someone had spread Speedy Dry, a substance car mechanics use to soak up oil spills, over the trail of Bangs's blood. The shotgun had mysteriously disappeared. The sergeant on the scene advised them to leave the barn so that the police could secure the area, and the four of them calmly picked up their coffee and walked downstairs. This was about the time Tommy called me to cancel our meeting.

As the three suspects were arrested down at Medford Police Station, the detective captain read them their rights and questioned them. They were all closemouthed. Remember, Tommy was a lieutenant on that force, a group known for its fanatical sense of brotherhood. At one point the captain said:

"Tom, if you'd like to say anything, I'll listen."

"I'd like to, but on the advice of my attorney I can't."

"Point me in a direction."

"Check the neighborhood," Tommy said, "and see how this guy's been acting. And look in the trunk of his car. I can say no more than that."

Near Bangs's car the police found a bloodstained plastic package of cocaine. As O'Malley told me and Brother the next morning, the troopers went into the trunk of the car and discovered the kilo of coke, the ten grand in Canadian bills, the guns and the jewelry. That jewelry was to turn out to be crucial to more than just this case. They also found photographs of Bangs dressed in women's clothing. (Troy would later say to Bangs in court that he "liked his summer wardrobe.")

But across the street, other interesting discoveries were taking place. In the barn, police found a lot of hot items from Tommy's career in petty crime, including some kitchen cabinets and drills. In Tommy's house they found four revolvers and two shotguns. But the most interesting discovery of all was made by State Police Detective Thomas Spartichino, the same man who had chased Vernon Gusmini down to Florida. While he was looking through Doherty's bookcase he came across a copy of a civil service exam that Doherty could not possibly have possessed legally. I had given that exam to Tommy the previous May, just before the exam was given, and like an idiot he had held onto it long after the exam was over.

That stolen exam was to have repercussions far beyond the Depositors Trust burglary, but my main concern following Tommy's release was to keep either him or Joe from turning on the other by bargaining for immunity and bringing the heist to light. There was no reason why either would have—except revenge or pure spite. It wouldn't help anybody involved to allow this thing to break wide open, especially with the statute of limitations closing in. So I became a conduit between Tommy and Joe, pacifying them, conveying offers, talking them out of acting rashly. As it turned out, Joe needed the majority of my attention.

After his stint in hospital, Joe went to Florida, where the state police kept him in protective custody. He called me regularly, but never told me where he was. Tommy, meanwhile, was back home, still dealing and still freebasing. With Joe in Florida, Tommy felt safe, but he still kept plenty of loaded weapons in the barn. Though Gillen went to jail on the Maine drug charge, Roberts and others were around, so Tommy didn't feel threatened. He still had his little empire in the barn.

Understandably, Joe wanted nothing more to do with Tommy. He did want the money he had lost, however, and also his half of the condo the two of them had bought the year before. I passed the information on to Tommy. Tommy said fine but did nothing. Fall passed into winter. Joe was brought before a grand jury but took the fifth. Flying back and forth between Florida and Boston, he would turn up unexpectedly on the doorstep of my house in Medford, baring his chest to show my wife and me his scars.

In December I met Joe and Brother at the Memory Lane Lounge in Somerville. I knew Brother was just as worried as I was about Joe and spent a lot of time with him. Joe's first question was about the condo.

"Has he sold the fucking thing or what?"

"He said you don't have to worry," I said.

Joe pointed at me with both forefingers.

"Look, Jerry, *you* buy the fucking thing. Burn it down and get the insurance. Steal his car—I don't give a shit. I want my share of the thing and I want the money he lost, simple as that."

"I'm only telling you what he told me."

"Well it ain't good enough, none of this shit is good enough. You're too soft on that son of a bitch—he tried to kill me, and you don't seem to remember that."

"I remember it, Joe, I remember."

"Well, you don't act like it. If that motherfucker had shot you I would've gone down to that barn and broken his fucking jaw. You're my friend and that's what I would've done for you. You should've done the same for me."

"You're right, Joe, you're 100-percent right."

"Now this son of a bitch is playing games while I—"

"Look," Brother interrupted, "we could talk about this all day but it won't get us anywhere."

"What the fuck are you worried about?" Joe said.

"I think," I said slowly, "that Brother—and me—are concerned about the heist being. . .being discussed, if you know what I mean."

"Hey, *I'm* not mentioning the thing, you understand? All I want is my money from Tommy. He'll get his day in court."

Since the grand jury appearance, Joe had cut a deal with the D.A., agreeing to testify about the shooting in exchange for immunity from drug charges stemming from the kilo found in his trunk. The troopers wanted Tommy badly.

"Anyway," Joe continued, "Tommy's the one you should be worried about. Did you know he wanted to take you and Barbara Hickey out?"

"Don't bullshit me, Joe."

"I'm not bullshitting, swear to God. He said you were the weak link and you had to go. He wanted me to do it."

I looked at Brother.

"Is this true?"

He nodded.

"Ask him," Joe said. "Just ask the motherfucker."

But what would be the point of asking Tommy? He would deny it. I didn't know who to believe anymore, and yet my position demanded that I know the truth. Brother would back Joe all the way—that was the way he was—but I was getting to where I needed Brother's help. Dealing with these two wackos was more than one man could handle.

During January and February there was a lot of drawn-out contact between Joe's lawyer and Tommy's lawyer. According to Joe, Tommy was to transfer money to Joe through the lawyers, and he was to make a deal on the condo. Joe's concerns revolved around two main points: that Tommy would stall on the cash, and that the condo would never get sold. As I've said, Joe was a silent partner in the property; his name was not on the deed, so there was no immediate legal way of getting his share. But he also had a lot of information on Tommy, information he could use to barter with. Because that included facts on the bank and the exams, my main concern was that the information would eventually broaden to include my own exploits.

According to Joe, Tommy agreed to give him what was called a quick claim deed, a legal document guaranteeing he was selling the property and entitling Joe to half the proceeds.

Since they were dealing exclusively through lawyers (no way was Tommy going to meet Joe face-to-face, or even talk to him on the phone), the process was laborious. Still, I thought we were getting somewhere—until someone threw a monkey wrench into the machinery.

Tommy did not want to sell the condo. Since he was concerned about paying his legal fee, he was worried about his financial position. Down the road, Tommy's remarks suggested, he saw that the condo might be his only way of paying his lawyers, so in May he conveniently ignored the deed deal and had a lien attached to the condo that would prevent its sale. I could see that Tommy was trying to have it both ways. Joe, who was on the edge at the best of times, went tumbling over when he heard this news. He called me and, high on coke, screamed into the phone:

"You've got five minutes to get your money out of the bank, Jerry, five fucking minutes, you hear me?"

"Joe, wait a minute..."

"This is the end of the fucking ballgame, Jerry, Tommy's out to stroke me. You got five minute to get an attorney, you understand? I'm going to the D.A."

He slammed the receiver home, leaving me to wonder what the hell was going on. I called Tommy, who told me about the lien. I said that I didn't want Joe and him bringing me down the tubes, but he insisted that the action was insignificant. He said he could get a quick claim deed tomorrow if that was what Joe wanted. I spent a sleepless night wondering what Joe was up to. In the morning I hooked up a recording device to my telephone. I was going to start looking out for my own interests.

Joe called again the next day. Though he was not as hyper as the day before, I could tell he was high.

"I'm just saying one thing, Jerry—protect yourself the best you can. It makes no difference to me now, because he's out to stroke me. Everything I know about that motherfucker I'm testifying to."

"Can I ask you a question? What's it got to do with, the coke thing?"

"It starts out with that and it goes into the other thing."

I assumed he was talking about Depositors Trust. Without actually saying it over the phone, Joe was constructing a scenario for me: he would take Tommy down on the coke dealing, for which Joe had immunity, and we would have to deal with the possibility of Tommy ratting on the bank job. He wanted to screw Tommy and pretend he himself was still a good guy.

"The only ones I'm naming are me, him and the other guy," Joe said. "If he names you people that's your fucking problem with him. If it was you, Jerry, you'd do the same, you know what I'm saying? And I wouldn't blame you one bit."

"Joe, I tried my damnedest with him, I really did. I mean, why the fuck should it cost me money?"

"If he involves you, that's your problem. If he can't get the money to me by Monday then I'm going to the FBI."

Here was a sliver of light. Now I knew Joe could be brought around.

"And once I get immunity," he said, "I ain't lying, I'm not committing perjury for anyone, you understand? That prick thinks he's calling my bluff? There was no fucking bluff involved, I'm 100-percent fucking serious. I'm going to have him by the fucking balls. Wait till they break that fucking thing with the exams."

"Why?" I said. "What's coming down with that?"

"He gave me that fucking exam. You don't think it has his fingerprints all over it?"

If that exam had Tommy's prints on it, it also had mine —I had given it to him.

"That exam stuff involves a lot more people than just Tommy."

"I don't give a fuck anymore, Jerry."

"Listen, if I can get a quick claim deed, will that satisfy you?"

He exploded again, yelling about how he was supposed to have that money six months ago.

"When this starts it's going to mushroom," he said, "I'm telling you now. And I'm guaranteed my piece of the action. You tell him, you tell him to meet me man-to-man in a field. We'll settle this between the two of us, no courts, no testimony, no nothing. He does that and I'll lie on the stand. I'll say I shot *myself* with a shotgun. But he doesn't have the balls."

"I tried to get your money, Joe, I tried."

"He's a liar. And I...this'll take everyone down, Jerry. I'm fucking ready."

"Joe, don't do anything stupid."

He breathed heavily for a few seconds. I let him calm down.

"And now he takes out a mortgage on that condo."

"It's not a mortgage, it's a lien. It doesn't mean anything."

He paused. He seemed to be cooling down a little.

"Look, call me Tuesday at twelve noon," he said. "If he gives you the money and the deed, then fine. And don't forget: twenty-four grand. He owes me twenty-four grand."

"I'll do the best I can," I said.

"This isn't extortion, Jerry. I just want what he owes me. Otherwise, if he wants to play dirty pool, fine. I can play dirty pool with the best of them."

"Just give me a little time."

"Twelve Tuesday."

I had three days. I got together with Brother and we approached Tommy. As usual, Tommy gave the impression he was more than cooperative. But we knew that Tommy was facing a trial for attempted murder, and we weren't sure if we could trust him. He still had that lien as well. After some uncomfortable conversation, Tommy suggested a deal that would avoid the condo altogether. He would come up with the $24,000 and half a kilo of coke, worth another $23,000, towards the condo. The condo was worth $82,000, so Joe's half came to $41,000. Tommy would owe him a balance of around $18,000, which he said he would pay in six to eight weeks. I would deliver the cash, Brother the coke—I wouldn't touch the drugs.

Over those three days I had three or four conversations a day with Joe. His tone ranged from reasonable to psychotic, depending on whether he had been freebasing or not. One day the deal was good enough; the next he wanted everything. He filled my tape recorder with more threats than I could list here. He still wanted Tommy to sell the condo and pay him in full, but eventually he agreed. Then Tommy could only come up with eighteen in cash—and he was short on the coke as well— so Joe ranted and raved about that for a while. What galled him the most was the idea of Tommy using the proceeds of the condo to pay for his defense. In effect, that would mean that Joe would be helping to pay for the lawyers defending the man who had shot him.

We transacted the deal at the lounge in the terminal of Delta Airlines, at Logan Airport, a day late. Brother brought the coke and I brought the money. Joe agreed to accept the other $6,000 and the remaining coke in two weeks, so I faced another extended period of hysterical phone calls and frantic peace-making. Then, to make matters worse, Brother refused to see Tommy anymore. Joe was running hot and cold with him, asking him to be a go-between at some times and giving him shit at others. So he wouldn't cooperate. That raised the problem of the coke; I was sticking to my policy of never going near the stuff, but there was no one else to deliver it. We talked for a while about Tommy putting the drugs into a locker at the airport, but Joe got cold feet. Finally, after several threatening calls from Joe, I agreed to bring him the money and the drugs. It was a last resort, a one-time agreement on my part. We agreed to meet at the same lounge in Logan.

I picked up the stuff, which Tommy had packaged in a cigar box, and drove to the airport. I was nervous. I sat at a table in the corner of the lounge and waited. Joe was late. After a few minutes I saw a state policeman, one of the plainclothes troopers attached to the D.A.'s office who were guarding Joe while he was in protective custody, walk in and sit down at the opposite side of the lounge. I knew the guy and he knew me, but he pretended not to recognize me. Oh shit, I thought, I'm being set up. Brother and Joe are tricking me into carrying the dope and I'm going to get busted. I wanted to get up and walk out right then, but I knew it wouldn't do any good. If he was going to bust me, he was going to bust me. So I hung tough.

Fifteen minutes later Joe arrived, a flurry of apologies and excuses.

"Sorry, Jerry, I just got off a plane. Flew up from Florida."

"Joe, look who's over there."

I mentioned the guy's name. Joe hardly glanced at him.

"That ain't him, just looks like him."

"Joe, I know who it is."

"You're wrong."

I made a point of giving the box to Joe at once. He put it into his briefcase and I breathed easier. I was clean now, but I still wondered why the trooper was there and why Joe pretended not to know him.

"Hey, let's get something to eat," Joe said.

We went out to a restaurant in East Boston. Half the time we were there, Joe was on the phone. I know now that he was setting up deals, that he had cruised in from Florida, where he had been in protective custody, to do a little dealing. The troopers who were guarding him, I also found out, were among his customers. According to Joe, the guy I had seen in the airport lounge used coke regularly. Joe also got hookers for him. Here were troopers getting paid overtime to watch a criminal, and they were partying away while he kept them in drugs. As for the trooper's presence at the airport, I have to assume that he was waiting for Joe, or that Joe led him to believe I was going to whack him. And it wasn't the last time I saw that guy either.

These deals may have temporarily patched things up between Joe and Tommy, but under the circumstances I didn't think it was wise to relax. As long as Joe continued his Jekyll-and-Hyde routine there was a danger that he would go all the way and rat on the bank. He saw enemies everywhere: he gave me constant shit for not punching Tommy and severing relations after the shooting, he was deaf to Brother's pleas for moderation, and he was so fickle in his attitude towards Brother's visits to Tommy that Brother just gave up trying to help long before I did. Dealing with him was like dealing with a psychotic.

Early in the summer I had hopes that Tommy's trial would be delayed a year, until the summer of 1986, when the state statute of limitations on the bank burglary would have run out. Tommy fueled my hopes by saying from time to time that he was going to fake a heart attack. He did have a heart condition that occasionally required him to be hospitalized. Joe led me to believe that he wanted the trial to be delayed as well. He repeatedly asked me about the trial, saying over and over that he wanted what was best for us all. But he was stroking me the whole time. Because he was working on the case with the prosecuting attorneys, he had the inside track on the trial dates himself. He knew more about it than I did, but he feigned ignorance so that he could conceal his own thoughts of betrayal. The last converstion I had with Joe before I stopped answering his calls was in early July, when he told me that the trial was starting on the fifteenth of that month.

"Yeah, I was with Carol Ball all afternoon," he said, referring to the assistant D.A. who was prosecuting Tommy, "and I'm going to crucify that son of a bitch. I'm going to gaff the motherfucker, you know what I'm saying?"

"Joe, all this could have been avoided."

"We got a serious problem here, Jerry. I've heard the things he's been saying. He said I came into the barn with a shotgun that night, can you believe that? He told a friend of mine that he's going to be a pallbearer at my funeral, at my fucking funeral. Well *fuck him*. He sold you down the tubes, he sold me down the tubes. The trial's going ahead, and I've got immunity."

"Joe, listen to me..."

"No, Jerry, you listen to me. He's turning on all of us and I'm not going to let him screw me. I don't want to fucking sandbag you, but this whole thing's gone beyond the point of no return. Simple as that. Payback is a bitch."

He hung up on me. I decided not to talk to him anymore. From that point on my wife screened my calls, and if Joe was on the phone she told him I wasn't home. In the meantime I hung tough—I'd weathered quite a few storms up to now, and even though this was a rough one I wasn't giving up hope. It still remained to be seen how far Joe was going to go with his testimony. I had heard nothing from my sources in the D.A.'s office to suggest that Joe was angling for immunity on the bank. And would he bring it up at Tommy's trial? Hardly.

The trial started in mid-July, but by the time jury selection and other proceedings were finished it was the beginning of August. I hadn't spoken to Joe in over a month, even though he called my house constantly. Joe took the stand on August 7, and his testimony lasted three days. He testified in minute detail to the events of the night of the shooting, the contents of the trunk of his car, his coke and marijuana deals with Tommy, his own use of coke, his freebasing, his relationship with Debbie O'Malley and other women, his junkets to Vegas and the Bahamas, the condo in Florida and the deterioration of his relationship with Tommy. There was plenty of fodder for the lawyers and the press.

But the biggest bombshell of all came when Troy, representing Doherty, asked Bangs where the jewelry found in his Cadillac had come from. Troy had been assured by the prosecuting team that the jewelry was legitimate, that it belonged to Bangs's ex-wife or ex-girlfriend. He was pursuing a line of questioning aimed at showing that nothing in the trunk had anything to do with Tommy—otherwise the jury might see the coke, money and jewelry as a motive for the shooting. Bangs's reply took everybody by surprise.

"Some of the jewelry was taken from a robbery Memorial Day weekend of Depositors Trust in Medford."

The courtroom was abuzz. While a couple of state troopers hurriedly left the courtroom, the judge called the attorneys to the bar and asked what was going on. Troy explained his reasons for asking the question. Then he moved for a mistrial, accusing prosecuting attorney Ball of setting him up.

"She had him primed to say something like that to inflame and prejudice this jury," Troy said heatedly.

Ball claimed that she was as surprised as anybody else.

"He has not received any immunity with regard to the Depositors Trust," Ball said.

"He's trying to get it right now," Troy countered.

The judge interposed.

"He has not received immunity for the bank. Ms. Ball says, as I understand it, there is no application for immunity for the bank. Let me just tell you one other thing—this particular problem arose from an excursion into the irrelevant."

The truth was, nothing could have been more relevant, especially for me, since that same day I heard that Joe had agreed to go before a federal grand jury and talk about the bank. If he hadn't received immunity for the heist by then, he received it very soon afterwards. Someone wasn't telling the whole story. And the biggest irony was that Joe was wrong—that jewelry had not come from the heist. In fact, Joe ended up getting the jewelry back after the trial. But the comment was certainly significant. I braced myself for the worst.

My wife and I went down to our bank the next day and withdrew all our savings, about $200,000, at the cost of $13,000 in penalties for early withdrawal. I wanted my money where I could see it. I had still not told her about my role in the robbery. I was not particularly worried because at this stage I knew that Joe's evidence would not be enough by itself to convict me. In a situation like this one involving immunity, corroborating testimony was required. And who could provide that? Barbara Hickey, that's who, but at the time I didn't dream that she would be a witness. I still felt that I would not be found out, even if I was indicted.

The state police began sitting outside my house. I had the Medford Police shake them down. Who are you? they asked. You know who the fuck we are, and so does he, they said, pointing at my house. But I wasn't going anywhere. Where would I go, anyway? Everything I had was here, everyone I knew. I had lived in Medford all my life, and if I wasn't here I was in Florida. I just sat and waited for the indictment to come down.

Joe kept calling me. He sent a message to me through my son—*fuck him*, he told Barry to tell me. I saw Joe's strategy—he threatened me to the point where I wouldn't talk to him and then used my silence as an excuse for giving me the shaft. I had never hurt him. I had never lied to him. I busted my ass to smooth things between him and Tommy, and in the end all I got for my trouble was an indictment. Not that I was the sole recipient of his nastiness—he turned on Brother, he turned on O'Malley, he even turned on the state police who were guarding him. They tolerated him only because of the information they were getting out of him. While he was in protective custody he would occasionally go crazy, smashing furniture and wrecking whatever house he was in. The guy was beyond reason.

Tommy's trial ended in late August. Al Roberts was found not guilty, but Gillen and Tommy were both found guilty of attempted murder, and Tommy was sentenced to eighteen to twenty years in state prison. The last time I ever spoke to Joe directly was the day of Tommy's sentencing. He called the house, and I listened on a second line while my wife answered the phone.

"Mary," Joe said, "I know he's not home, so here's a message..."

I cut in.

"I'm home."

"The state police are listening in," he said, "so this isn't a threatening phone call. I talked to Brother already...like I told you last time, I said let the cards fall where they fall."

He was so high on coke I could hardly understand him.

"What cards?" I said. "I don't even know what the fuck you're talking about."

"Don't say anything incriminating, Jerry. You know what I'm talking about. I was at the airport, OK? I sandbagged you. Just keep that in mind—you were sandbagged at the airport."

"For what, giving you money?"

"No, when you gave me money, you gave me drugs. Don't answer, Jerry, don't incriminate yourself over the phone. They're listening."

He may have been trying to get me to say something incriminating by bullying me, or he may have been bluffing about the state police, trying to scare me and making the point that he was gaffing me. Or he could have even meant that the drugs I'd delivered were meant for the troopers who were guarding him—as if I'd care. At any rate I knew that if I was going to get busted for that delivery it would have had to have happened at the time. The guy was so coked up he was making no sense. He descended to screaming threats.

"Fuck you, Jerry, you're a fucking rat and so isn't fucking..."

"*I'm* a rat?" I said.

"You're a fucking ratfink."

"Cut the shit."

"Jerry, you're a fucking rat, you sandbagged me from the go."

"I sandbagged you?"

"You didn't answer my fucking calls. Three weeks I looked for you. Fuck you, Clemente. I'll testify in court."

He was screaming at the top of his voice now.

"That's why I turned on you...get every fucking word you can get."

"What?"

He hung up. This is the Joe Bangs I think of now—not the guy I trusted in the past, not the smooth-talking witness on the stand, not the calculating hood, but the hyper, coked-up, distrusting, name-calling liar he turned into after his two-year-long ride on freebased cocaine. Who would have thought it would come to this?

There was nothing left to do but sit in my house in Medford, staring down the troopers outside and waiting, as Joe might say, for the cards to fall where they would.

10

For the Man Who Has Everything but. . .

When I heard Joe had gone before the grand jury, I knew I was going to be indicted. He had already told them everything he could about the shooting, so it didn't take a genius to figure out what his next topic of interest would be for the authorities, especially after his final phone call to me. But even knowing what was inevitable, I did not lose my cool. If anything I became more calculating—I had to, since the odds had turned from being in my favor to being against me. Besides all of the usual authorities pursuing me, I now had Bangs as an enemy as well, so I had to turn my attention from trying to save the gang to trying to save my ass.

Tommy was a lost cause anyway. He got eighteen to twenty for his unsuccessful attempt on Joe's life, and since he still faced time for his botched drug deal down in Mississippi in 1984, I knew there would be August snowstorms in Miami before he saw the light of the free world again. But I didn't waste much sympathy on him; he more than anyone was responsible for the chain of events that led to Joe's craziness and betrayal, and during the remaining months of 1985, as the D.A. marshaled his forces and I waited for my indictment to come down, I often cursed Tommy and Joe and the cocaine that made them forget how much we had at stake and how close we were to beating the statute of limitations.

It is difficult to describe my state of mind at this point. Obviously I was nervous—I stood to lose my freedom and all I owned, after all—but I still had my confidence and my resolve. I've been asked since then if I did not feel guilty or

remorseful for what I had done, but even though I can see
now, after all the dust has settled, how greed and corruption
had blinded me completely, I still understand that the criminal
mentality simply does not view the world in terms of justice
and retribution. For me, the impending indictment and trial
were like a game, where I would match wits with the authorities
pursuing me and do my best to use the American legal system
to my advantage. As I saw it, those were the rules, and I was
going to do my damnedest, through the courts if necessary,
not to get caught.

Joe went into protective custody on August 21, the day
before Doherty and Gillen were convicted, and on September
11 he was granted immunity for the Depositors Trust burglary,
the planned burglary of the state treasury, all of his cocaine
and marijuana trafficking and any possible crimes relating to
the theft of civil service exams. If you stacked up the years
that Joe should have got for his drug offenses alone, you
would have had enough time to put a whole gang away for
life, so he was definitely getting a bargain, even if he did sell
me, Tommy, Kenny and his best friend Brother down the river.

Joe's opening grand jury appearance was the following day,
September 12. He testified at length about the burglary, including specific details of the planning, break-in and distribution of money. He gave a night-by-night description of the
proceedings that included information about tools, transpor-
tation, equipment and alibis. For the most part he told the
truth, though he did introduce some significant discrepancies
that made me appear to be the mastermind of the heist. He
said I suggested breaking into the Depositors Trust, when it
was in fact Tommy who did so. He said I had blueprints of
the bank vault when, to my knowledge, no such blueprints
existed outside of Vernon Gusmini's imagination. He had me
outside the vault, directing operations, when in reality I was
inside the vault during most of the heist, sweating alongside
the others and following Bucky's directions. If anyone was
the mastermind it was Bucky Barrett, who, by the time Joe

came to testify, had been conveniently missing and presumed dead for nearly three years. He was the one with knowledge and experience. He was the one who told us what to do and what precautions to take. I did what he suggested. Joe knew this as well as anybody, but for reasons of spite or pressure by the investigating authorities (who were galled that a captain in the Metropolitan Police should be engaged in such activities), he decided to alter the truth.

But these lies grew even larger as Bangs went on to testify about the years following the burglary. He said that it was I who suggested Barbara Hickey be killed or have her house burned down, when it was actually he himself who had made the offer. He made me out to be a violent man, when he was the most violent of us all. I was the level-headed one when things got hot; I was the one who held things together when the others wanted to take people out; I was the one who watched passively while the others got deeper and deeper into the violent world of drugs and organized crime. Joe was the guy beating his girlfriend and pistol-whipping her ex-boyfriends. Joe was the guy selling kilos of coke that he bought with that part of the robbery I never even got near. Joe was the guy screaming threats into the phone as his world fell apart. Yet now he was painting me as the ringleader of the gang, and a violent one at that. It was bad enough getting caught—it was even worse being blamed for more than I had actually done.

I turned out to be the primary target of that grand jury. Tommy was already behind bars, and Brother and Kenny were considered small fry compared to an ex-cop. In fact, Brother was brought before the grand jury himself, though he took the fifth all the way. My son, Barry, was also called, as well as a number of Medford cops and investigating officers. But Joe was the main man, the source of the only first-hand evidence against me—a situation that concerned the investigators. They knew (and I knew) that Joe's testimony was enough to get me indicted, but would it be enough to convict me? I didn't think so, which is why I was still confident. After all, the D.A. was saddled with a main witness of very shaky credibility: a self-confessed burglar, thief and cocaine dealer who had admitted to dealing drugs while in the protective custody of state police. He knew he would have to find someone who could corroborate Joe's story, and there was no one. At least I thought there was no one, but when the time came the D.A. knew exactly where to look.

Barbara Hickey had been out of my life for three years. I had not seen her since our break-up in December 1982, and I had no desire ever to see her again. Since her grand jury appearances in 1982, however, I knew that she had received a number of visits from federal and state law enforcement officials who spent a lot of time trying to convince her that her memory of my comings and goings over the 1980 Memorial Day weekend might be a little faulty. I tried to monitor her movements and phone calls by watching her house and bugging her phone, but I wasn't particularly worried. I had never mentioned the robbery to her; in six years I didn't even tell my own wife and son. My pattern of visiting Barbara over that crucial weekend had been no different from my previous visits, so I didn't see how she could come up with anything that would corroborate Bangs's testimony. As far as I knew, in the three years following our break-up, she had told the authorities nothing.

But as the extent of Bangs's testimony became apparent and the grand jury hearings stretched into October and November, the D.A.'s office put pressure on her. At some point she changed her story. The prosecution told her that she had perjured herself, and that she could be tried for it if she didn't testify. They offered her immunity if she testified against me. This was all happening behind the scenes, of course, and I didn't find out about it until later. But when I heard she was in the hot seat I wasn't too happy. I knew how expert these guys were in interrogation, how they could spin your head and put words into your mouth. I found out soon enough that

Barbara finally confessed to them that she had committed perjury before the grand jury in 1982 and that I had told her I had robbed the bank. Naturally I was crestfallen. That was not how I had remembered events.

Another thing that worried me was news that Barbara had finally gotten a job in the judicial system. When I was seeing Barbara she was constantly asking me about getting her a job in court. She didn't want a typist's job, however; she wanted to start at the top. All these years she had been unsuccessful in her quest, so when I heard about her new position I became suspicious. Was it possible, I asked myself, that the D.A. dangled a job in front of her as bait? I don't know if I was right, but on Thanksgiving Day 1985 she agreed to go before the grand jury. She was the last to testify, and the things she said, which she was to repeat at length during my trial, led directly to my indictment.

But in the meantime the law was trying to nail me from another angle. The more I had to worry about, they figured, the easier I'd be to collar. A friend of mine, a former Metropolitan cop, had been illegally selling semiautomatic machine guns from the basement of his house. He had managed to get hold of six Mac 10 machine pistols, valuable guns that the government had banned some years ago because they were so easily convertible to automatic weapons. Of his six, this guy sold two to Tommy, two to me and kept two for himself. I gave one back, and my friend, in a move that came back to haunt him, resold it to another Metropolitan cop.

The feds had been after his ass for years. They knew he was dealing Mac 10s, but couldn't prove it. They were also after my ass through this guy, since they knew he was my friend. In 1984 the Bureau of Alcohol, Tobacco and Firearms subpoenaed his records. He was a licensed dealer who, in addition to his illegal activities, had legitimately sold weapons to a lot of local people, including a number of Medford cops. The bureau men visited many of these people, trying to nail him—but they were after more than that. I heard from some of the guys they'd approached that they were asking questions about the bank. I also knew it was only a matter of time before they got to me, as I had bought legitimately registered guns from my pal as well. In order to avoid the kind of word-twisting that followed my last meeting with feds at my house, I set up a tape recorder at the front door and waited for them to come by.

They arrived in December, the day before I was going to Florida. I answered the door and they identified themselves.

"Hello gentlemen," I said. "For your protection—and mine—I'm going to record our conversation. That way nothing either of us says can be misconstrued."

As I said this I hit the record button. They looked on, nonplussed.

"Well, we have a—some records that we've been examining, and your name appears as having purchased a couple of firearms." They mentioned my friend's name. "We're trying to verify that."

"In other words," I said, "you're going to screw a cop and you want me to help you, is that it?"

"All we want to do is verify whether you bought the guns."

"What kind of guns?"

"Two of them. One's a Charter Arms Explorer Two, .22 caliber pistol, and the other's a Charter Arms Explorer rifle."

"Correct."

"Did you buy both of them?"

"Yes I did."

"Thank you very much. That's all."

That was it. They left, obviously pissed that they couldn't ask me about the bank. Unfortunately, it made them more determined than ever to get me through this guy, so when they finally did bust him less than a year later, they really put the squeeze on him, hoping that they could pin a big purchase on me, indict me and bring me around on the bank. My friend rolled over, lying before a grand jury. He said I had bought five guns, and he even claimed that I had forged all the forms necessary to make the transaction look legal. His claims were enough for an indictment, which I received in October. But I never did go to trial. Before anything could happen a chain of events that took precedence over everything began. After getting Barbara Hickey's testimony the D.A. judged he had enough evidence to move, and on December 9 the law closed in on me.

At six-thirty in the morning the state police arrived at my house, a crew of television cameramen in tow. They knocked at my door and my wife stuck her head out our bedroom window to see who was there. But before anyone said anything I knew who was visiting. I got out of bed and pulled on my pants, throwing my wallet into the bureau. Anything I had with me would be taken, scrutinized and photographed, so I wanted to go clean. At the door the troopers handed me the warrant, frisked me, handcuffed me and led me out to the police car under the glare of television lights. Among them I recognized the same policeman I had seen out in Logan Airport when I delivered Joe the money and coke, the same guy Joe had said he had supplied with hookers and drugs. This was what it had come to—one corrupt cop picking up another. I may have been the one being arrested, but I had no illusions about the whole process. Today it was me; tomorrow it would be him.

"Don't you want your wallet?" a trooper asked after frisking me.

"What would I need it for?"

He shrugged.

"Am I going to get bail?"

"You'll be the only one able to afford it," he said.

So news of my $200,000 withdrawal was out. I knew I could count on a high bail.

We drove off as television reporters shouted questions. I sat silently in the back of the car with my wife, staring at the cold streets stained blue by the swiveling lights of the cruiser. As we made our way through the dark winter morning I thought back to those warm May mornings five and a half years ago, when I had driven along these same streets with tens of thousands of dollars in my trunk and visions of millions in my head. I had come a long way since then. I had seen those millions disappear into the clutches of Bucky Barrett and Joe Bangs. I had seen Joe and Tommy disintegrate before my very eyes. I had come to a point where I could depend on no one but myself. But I still had hope. They still had to try me.

The police brought me to the D.A.'s office in the city of Cambridge and locked me in a holding cell in the building's basement. This was to be my home for the next three months. After an hour or so on my own I was joined by Brother O'Leary and Kenny Holmes, dour-faced and taciturn, who were placed in cells adjacent to mine. It was the first time I had seen Kenny since the heist, when I knew him as Charley. Now I found out his real name as we renewed our acquaintance. We had to be careful when we spoke; after all, we had no way of knowing each other unless we were guilty. Brother and I said hello and complained carefully about Joe, but at this point neither of us knew what was going to happen.

Later that day we were arraigned in Middlesex Superior Court. Tommy was brought in from prison and the next day all the Boston-area papers featured a photograph of Tommy, Kenny, Brother and me sitting together, bleakly gazing into space as we listened to the judge set an outrageously high bail of two million dollars—$200,000 cash. Not coincidentally, the figure matched what I had withdrawn from my bank account three and a half months ago. The court wanted that cash in their clutches. Referring to Bangs's grand jury testimony, the assistant D.A. argued at length that I was a violent man and implied I had threatened witnesses. So the bail was set so high I would have had to sink every penny I had into it if I wanted to be free until the trial.

The four of us pleaded innocent to charges of breaking and entering, larceny over a hundred dollars and conspiracy. I did not fork out the bail because I feared I would never see the money again, and I would not have been able to pay my lawyers. For a time I considered going after a big-name lawyer—a William Kunstler or an F. Lee Bailey or a local guy like James St. Clair of the law firm that defended Nixon—but in the end I stuck with Marty Weinberg and his partner, Joe Oteri. The others were out of my range financially. As it was, I ended up using my entire share of the bank proceeds to pay for my representation.

As a result of the high bail I had to remain in that tight cell in Cambridge and build my case with all the strictures that it entailed: the difficulties of trying to see people, the reluctance of lawyers to visit me, the constant presence of guards, the discomfort. It was not going to be easy.

I spent a lot of time on the phone with Weinberg and Oteri, building strategy and planning procedure. We hired a CPA to prove that my financial situation was such that I need not have robbed a bank to have the money I did. We talked about cross-examining Bangs and Hickey. It was tough doing all this while I was inside, but it had to be done. In the meantime the prosecutors were playing their part of the game as well. They approached all of us individually with offers of immunity. I can still remember their approach.

"We have one more white hat to give away, Clemente. Do you want it?"

"I don't need it."

"C'mon, why don't you talk to us?"

"Nothing to talk about. I didn't do it."

They offered Kenny and Brother similar deals. Brother, who was after all a friend of Joe from way back, also refused. Later he told me why:

"Jerry, I have to get up in the morning and look at myself in the mirror."

I believed him, especially as the D.A. and his cronies were constantly on him to roll over. They figured he knew more than Kenny, including information on the stealing of civil service exams they wanted to use to nail me. We all had our little roles to play in the game. We all waited and watched and plotted.

I had never been in jail before, and it took some getting used to. Apart from the general, depressing feeling of being locked in, there were all sorts of minor discomforts, ranging from an uncomfortable bunk to noncontact visits in the meeting room, where you were separated from your visitor by a sheet of plate glass. I talked a lot with Kenny, whispering when the guards were out of earshot. He spoke at length about Bucky, about their background together, about Bucky's disappearance. He told me about his life of crime and how he'd never got caught until this time. The police had found some safebreaking equipment in the basement of his mother-in-law's house, but more importantly they discovered the Movado watch he had taken from the stash for his wife. It was a conclusive piece of evidence. Kenny also complained bitterly about Joe. For a gang member to rat on another was to him the worst sin.

My lawyers successfully argued that I should be tried apart from the other gang members. Unlike Brother and Kenny, I was not a professional criminal. Unlike Tommy and Joe, I had never had anything to do with drugs or attempted murder. We knew that the prosecution would depend on the testimony of Bangs and Hickey to try to convict me. We also knew the prosecution was worried, otherwise they would not be offering immunity to me, Brother or Kenny. I was confident that a jury would find neither Bangs nor Hickey credible witnesses. Bangs's criminal background would make him suspect from the start. To me, Hickey, now claiming she had perjured herself many times over the last five years, looked like a jilted lover getting revenge. As far as I was concerned, my incarceration was temporary.

By the time the trial began on March 3, 1986, I was eager to get on with it. I was tired of jail and eager to get home. I really expected to be cleared of all charges and back in my Medford house within a week, two weeks at the outside. I was playing the part of an innocent man, even to the extent of not telling my wife about my role in the burglary.

The trial attracted a good deal of media attention. All the local newspapers and television stations were there from day one, and with television cameras allowed in the courtroom, the proceedings made their way into living rooms throughout the greater Boston area.

The prosecution didn't waste any time; they called Joe to the stand as their first witness on March 6. He sat there for three straight days of direct testimony and cross-examination while the cameras recorded his careful replies. The prosecution had prepared him well, interviewing him, briefing him and outlining specifically what they would ask and how he would answer; hundreds of hours they worked on him while spending hundreds of thousands of dollars on his protective custody.

Joe had an odd, studied way of sucking at his teeth as he replied. He answered all questions slowly and methodically. I couldn't help but marvel at the complete contrast between this placid man on the stand and the hyper, drugged, threatening guy who had screamed into my phone so recently. It was a revelation. It gave me a look into Joe's soul. I had known the man for years, for years he had been my friend, but only in betrayal did he reveal his full character.

It did not take Bangs long to tell his first lie. After speaking briefly about his own history and his relationship with me, he described the incident where he and Brother disposed of my Cadillac in 1979. He said that after that incident I said I owed him a favor. He said that he approached me soon afterwards with news that he had an alarm man.

"After telling Mr. Clemente that you had located an alarm man," the prosecuting attorney asked, "what did he say to you?"

"Captain Clemente stated to me that...if the man is that good at alarm systems, that he has the blueprints of a bank in the city of Medford."

"And did he give you the name of that bank?"

"Yes, he did."

"And what was the name of that bank?"

"Depositors Trust."

I sat beside my attorney and stared at Joe. He knew as well as I did that his shitcanning my car had nothing to do with the bank and that those blueprints never existed. He knew as well as I that Tommy had suggested doing the bank. For some reason, telling the truth was not enough; he wanted to paint me as the mastermind as well. And his comments made the headlines of every news broadcast in Boston that evening. As I sat and looked at him I tried to channel all my malice into my gaze. But he did not then, nor at any other time during the trial, look me in the eye.

Joe spent the rest of that day describing the preparation we had made for the heist and the night of the break-in. He related how he and Brother had skimmed cash off the top, how Kenny had asked if he could take the Movado watch he wanted and what we all did that first night. He'd been prepared, all right.

Ten o'clock the next morning Joe was back on the stand, going through the details of the second and third nights we were in the vault as well as the events immediately following the heist. He said, falsely, that I was given the diamonds and precious stones to keep, though he also claimed I handed them back to him after my brush with the FBI. But it was when the prosecutors got him onto the subject of Barbara Hickey that the lies really started to flow.

"What did Mr. Clemente tell you about Barbara Hickey and his alibi?" Joe was asked.

"He told me that he was getting worried about Barbara Hickey, that there was a lot of pressure on her from the FBI and testimony in the grand jury or whatever. And he was scared, well, not scared—strike that—he was *concerned* that she would tell a different story of him...that she would go to the authorities with information of his activities, and he suggested or asked me if I would kill Barbara Hickey for him."

Over my lawyers' objections this line of testimony continued, with details of Barbara's confusion, the proposed burning of her house and other lies filling the jury's ears. I sat and stared, my only consolation the possibility that the jury would not believe him. Inside I felt anger and fear, though I had not lost my confidence.

After lunch Marty Weinberg began his cross-examination of Bangs. Attacking his credibility, he asked Bangs questions that exposed the long hours of preparation he had spent with the prosecution, how much Bangs stood to gain by turning against me and the extent of his drug activity. Weinberg drew attention to the fact that the ten grand in Canadian bills and the jewelry found in the trunk of his car had been returned to Joe. He got Joe to admit to having grossed millions of dollars as a result of marijuana trafficking alone. He rode him hard on the details of his background in drugs, drawing particular attention to the years in prison he escaped by bargaining for immunity. After one heated period of grilling, the court took a ten-minute break. Troopers surrounded Joe, and as I stretched my legs in front of the bench I heard him say:

"You don't know what the fuck you're doing, Clemente."

Weinberg continued pressing Bangs about drugs after the break, and at three-thirty testimony concluded for the day. Back in my jail cell in Cambridge, Brother and Kenny asked me for information, and I related all Joe had said. Brother avoided my eyes when I mentioned Joe's testimony about them skimming cash off the top of the duffel bags, but at that point I didn't care. I just wanted the ordeal over with.

That was a Friday, so I had to wait over the weekend for the conclusion of Bangs's testimony. It was a long couple of days. During the hours when we were allowed out of the cells, I held strategy sessions with Brother and Kenny, going over testimony so that they would be better prepared for their trials. On Monday cross-examination continued, and Weinberg re-created, through his questions and Bangs's responses, the situation that led to my refusing to talk to Joe and Joe's anger with me. He wanted to show the jury that Bangs was mad enough at Tommy and me, Tommy's friend, to lie about us on the stand. Joe did lie, of course, but he also told the truth about a good deal of the heist. I knew we had an uphill battle.

But we still felt that Joe's lack of credibility was in our favor—and we were right. Long after the trial was over, I heard through the grapevine that the jurors would not have convicted me on Bangs's evidence alone. Barbara Hickey's testimony is what swung them. Barbara came to the stand on March 11, the day after Joe had completed his testimony. As I had done with Joe, I looked her square in the eyes the whole time. Like Joe she never looked back at me. She began by stating that she was "currently employed as a court officer in Middlesex Superior Court." (She lost that job the month after the trial ended.) She proceeded to identify me and describe the history of our relationship.

Barbara's testimony did not take me by surprise; my lawyers had told me what was coming. But she did make me angry. Her version of those few days in 1980 and what preceded them did not jibe with mine. I was suspicious of the many minor details she remembered, especially as she had told state troopers investigating the crime that her memory of events that happened so long ago was hazy. Of course, my lawyers pointed this out, but that did not stop me being angry when I heard her on the stand. The prosecutor prompted her to reveal a conversation that reputedly took place before the Memorial Day weekend in 1980, for example, to which she replied:

"We were watching TV, and out of the clear blue sky he said that he was going to have a lot of money and he would never have to work a day in his life again."

I did not remember saying anything remotely resembling those words. I stared at her. Though nothing may have been showing on the outside, I was seething inside.

"What did you say?" the prosecutor asked.

"I said, 'Well, how would you get a lot of money without working a day, you know, a day in your life, you know, again?' And he said that it had something to do with a bank."

"What did you say?"

"I asked him what bank. And he said, 'You'll read about it in the newspaper.' "

She was just getting warmed up. She went on to say that when I met her at the baseball field in Revere the Sunday of that weekend, when I had been working on my boat, I told her I had been drilling at the bank. She said that some telephone plugs I had used for work on her mother's phone were in fact blasting caps I had used in the bank, brought to her house and thrown into the ocean. She said that I had her sign a statement about my presence in her house that was untrue. On and on she went. She claimed that I told her Tommy, Joe, Brother and I had done the job. She did not mention Bucky or Kenny—because she did not know them. Now, if I had told her about the job, why would I omit those two? To my mind, the inconsistencies piled up, and the more I listened, the angrier I got. Remember, I was playing a game, and I expected everybody to play by the rules. I had broken the rules, sure, but I wanted to get away with it. I was a criminal. Remember too that I had known Barbara intimately for four years. She had been, I thought, a friend, and the same sense of betrayal that I felt with Joe welled up in me now with her. My freedom was on the line and she was helping the prosecution.

The prosecution finished with Barbara mid-morning, and my lawyer, Joe Oteri, took over, cross-examining her for the rest of the day. He zeroed in on her desire for a court job and her supposed record of perjury. She said she lied right up to August 1985, by which time she was obviously not trying to protect me. Her testimony suggested that she had made a sudden decision to cooperate, a decision that seemed to me to coincide with her job as a court officer and her awareness of Joe's accusations.

Listening to Barbara was like reliving a portion of my life
I wanted to forget. She talked about our relationship. She
talked about our falling-out and her attempts at convincing
me to get a divorce. But as she related it, I was the one who
wanted a divorce.

"He's the one who wanted to go," she said.

"Did he get a divorce?"

"He said he wanted a divorce, but he didn't—"

"Did he get a divorce, ma'am?"

"No he didn't."

"Were you upset?"

"No, I wasn't upset."

"You were happy he didn't get a divorce?"

"No I wasn't happy, but I wasn't upset."

But I knew her better than anyone there. I could see beneath
the calm exterior, and I knew even now she was irritated. If
Barbara was anything she was tough, and she did not give in
easily—her testimony now proved that. Oteri persisted.

"He wanted the divorce?"

"He said he did."

"But he never got it."

"I don't know why."

"You were disappointed?"

"Well, I was kind of disappointed about him telling me he
was going to do something but never stuck by his word."

"Five years you were with him, right?"

"Five years. Five years he lied."

"Five years he lied," Oteri repeated.

Oteri turned to his desk and picked up a paper bag.

"Your honor, may I approach the bench?"

"Yes sir."

Oteri slowly walked to the witness stand.

"I want to show you something, ma'am, and ask if you
recognize this."

"Just put it down," the judge interposed, "and then step
back, and then you can ask her."

"I have to get something out of it, sir."

He reached slowly into the bag. The courtroom seemed filled with curiosity.

"Do you recognize—"

"I said no questions while you're there."

The whole courtroom was straining to see what the attorney had placed in front of her. I knew, of course, that the object was a pair of styrofoam balls that Barbara had sent after our break-up, accompanied by a special message.

"Do you recognize that?"

Barbara looked distinctly uncomfortable.

"That was supposed to be a joke."

Everyone was trying to get a look at the exhibit.

"May I go back, your honor, and show the—mark the exhibit?'

The prosecuting attorney was leaning forward, trying to get a look at the balls.

"Can I see it?" he said.

"Sure," Oteri said. "I'm going to show you now."

The judge jumped in again.

"Well, all the testimony I've heard—she said it was a joke. You'd better ask her a few more questions."

"OK. This is a joke," Oteri said. "You sent Jerry Clemente at some time a pair of balls and a note that says *For the man who has everything but.*"

The courtroom audience tittered.

"Is that correct?"

"Right."

"That's what you thought of Jerry Clemente?"

"Because," she said, "he lied so."

The attorney picked up his papers and moved back to our desk as the audience hushed.

"No further questions, your honor."

Oteri's interchange with Hickey left me feeling confident. I felt certain that the jury would see her as a former lover who could not be counted on for credible testimony. The little game that my own lawyer had played had a very dramatic effect on the jury. At least that was how it seemed to me. I couldn't see how either Bangs or Hickey could be believable to the twelve people sitting to my right—but then I was trying like hell myself to believe what I wanted to happen. I had everything at stake.

For all intents and purposes, the trial was over. There was one more day of testimony, most of it regarding my financial situation and whether it could or could not have come about unless I'd had an illegal source of income. The prosecution called some Boston police to the stand to testify to the discovery of the Movado watch in Kenny's mother-in-law's house (entirely irrelevant in my case); my own lawyers called my kid brother and some bank officials to attest to my financial status. But the witnesses who counted, the two who were going to make me or break me, had had their say. It was time to wait.

The jury began deliberations on Thursday, March 13. By the end of Friday they had still not come to a decison, and my attorney told me: "You're going home." He figured that deliberations of that length would have to end in either a hung jury or a decision in my favor. I called my wife Friday night and told her to expect me soon.

The weekend crawled by and deliberations resumed Monday. Still no decision, and I felt more confident than ever. Tuesday, March 18, 1986, the jury met for their fourth day. After three hours they reappeared in the courtroom with their decision. I sat beside my lawyers, my elbows on the desk and my hands at my chin. Television cameras whirred at the rear of the chamber. Newspaper cameramen stood with their cameras posed, ready to capture my reaction. The jury filed in as if in slow motion. The judge asked the foreman if the jury had reached a verdict. Yes, they had. Just a formality, I thought to myself, just a formality.

What happened over the course of the next few mintues did not seem real to me then and still seems like a dream to this day. I was found guilty, of course, on all counts. But the judge hit me with a double whammy by sentencing me then and there. After a lengthy speech during which he lambasted me for all he was worth, he dropped a second bombshell: he gave me eighteen to twenty years for burglary and twelve to twenty for two counts of breaking and entering—the optical shop and the bank—a total of thirty to forty years in jail. Though I didn't hear him at the time, he told me that I was a disgrace to the community and that I shouldn't even think about trying to get my sentence revised or revoked without first cooperating with the government on the civil service exams.

In a daze, I listened. I had never heard of anyone getting so steep a sentence for a nonviolent crime, done by someone with no criminal record. The courtroom seemed to spin around me—the world was a jangle of unintelligible words and unsympathetic faces. Somehow I managed to file out of the courtroom and into an antechamber. My attorney was speaking to me, but I didn't hear a word he said. The last few minutes had not sunk in.

"What does this mean?" I asked Weinberg.

"Thirty to forty? A minimum of ten years."

Ten years. A decade of my life.

"When does it...when does it start?"

A trooper looked over at me.

"Starts tonight, pal."

They didn't even allow me to return to my cell and pick up my stuff. Without further ado, I was whisked out to Walpole, the toughest, meanest high-security prison in Massachusetts. I was disoriented, shocked and completely unprepared for what I would face out there. After a series of gruff, bureaucratic confrontations with iron-faced prison staff, I was led to a large holding area divided into cells and placed in one of the cells. The other prisoners knew who I was and why I was there; they had seen the television news that week. They started yelling.

"Hey, you cop motherfucker."

"Bring him over here, bring him over here."

"We're going to fuck you up the ass, you piece of shit."

Food started flying across from the adjoining cells: cartons of milk, pieces of fruit, slices of bread. I sat at the end of my bunk and tried to close my ears. I was scared. I was overwhelmed. All I could think of were the horror stories that I'd heard about cops in Walpole. I had never spent a night in prison in my life, and now I was faced with the prospect of ten years of this abuse. I sat and waited and watched the splattered milk run down the cell wall. My slide down the chute of corruption was complete.

Epilogue

I'll never get used to prison. But I have, in the year I've served so far, resigned myself to what happened and learned a lesson or two on the way. I broke the law and the law caught me. Now I'll do my time. Those are the rules, and whatever I think of Joe Bangs or Barbara Hickey won't change that. Whatever I feel about the severity of my sentence I may as well keep to myself, because the cold hard fact is that I was a renegade cop who got busted. All the luxuries I tried so hard to get for myself are now denied me, all the illegal privileges I gained are now gone. I have to make do with what prison has to offer, and prison doesn't offer much of anything except time. Time to think back over the years. Time to review the way I acted. Time to ask myself a few questions.

Why did I help burgle the Depositors Trust? Why did I help plan the break-in of the state treasury two years later? Why, over the course of the last decade, did I steal civil service exams, sell them at three grand a pop, and keep going back for more? I certainly didn't need the money. Had I scrupulously avoided every one of my illegal activities over the years, my financial situation would still have been more than adequate. I had a good job, a nice home, a supportive family—a secure life. Something drove me beyond those basics.

I've spent a lot of time trying to figure out what that something was. Over the course of this book I've often said that greed was the force that drove me into crime, but one of the things I've realized while in prison is that greed only partly explains my actions. The real reasons for my behavior are far more complicated than that. They reach back to my years on the Medford police, to the time when I first learned the link between being corrupt and being accepted. The real reasons are to be found in that tangle of authority and privilege in public life that turns so easily into corruption. I took that route to its logical conclusion. Where others may have stopped because of fear or lack of nerve or conscience, I kept going. I completed the equation.

I possessed a combination of power and lack of conscience that was extremely dangerous. A man who wears a badge holds an authority that can wreak havoc if he does not have a clear sense of right and wrong. That badge becomes a shield for the illegal instead of a symbol of protection. With my own sense of justice as muddied as it was, I was in that dangerous position for years. I could wander around the state office buildings downtown, breaking into desks and safes and checking out the treasury, secure in my knowledge that, if I got caught, my badge and my wits would save me. Tommy used the same shield of authority to help us break into the Depositors Trust. In this position, greed and corruption feed on each other, and as time passes each becomes hungrier. I was caught in a vicious circle, and it was only a matter of time before the circle closed in on me.

With this warped view of authority, I was incapable of seeing my actions for what they were. I saw the burglary as an opportunity to make money, but I also saw it as an adventure. I enjoyed the excitement and the danger. As I saw my trial years later, I looked at my adventures as little games. I had moral blinkers on.

Removing those blinkers has enabled me to see not only my own actions for what they were, but also the huge extent to which our police system has become corrupt. Larceny, drugs, graft, conspiracy—I saw enough of these crimes over my twenty-four years as a policeman to know that corruption is not a series of isolated incidents but a far-reaching problem that leaves no city in the country untouched. The code of honor among police, the brotherhood that refuses to recognize corruption when it sees it, only deepens the problem. And I am not talking about diehard criminals here—I sold exams to men of every kind of temperament and background, many of whom, in different circumstances, would never have dreamed of doing something illegal. But who, when presented with the option of studying for years and possibly getting nowhere, and paying three grand and being assured of success and promotion, can resist? The opportunity, when it presents itself, is very attractive, especially when you can be nearly certain that your peers, even if they are straight, won't rat on you. I can understand its appeal. But I can also see how it needs to be rooted out.

I see the same thing here in prison. I wasn't here for a week before I was approached by fellow inmates wanting to know what I needed. Heroin? Coke? Special privileges? If you had the money, anything could be obtained. The corrections officers were just like the police—a significant number of them had yielded to temptation. They saw that money could be made out of their position illegally, so they went for it. And it is common knowledge that every prison in the nation is a country in itself, governed by the whims of the guards, complete with underground economy and ruling hierarchy. But I have learned my lesson. I steer clear of it all.

There is some sign that times are changing. The old guard, with its code of silence and fanatical sense of brotherhood, is beginning to be replaced by a younger corps of police administrators eager to bring corruption to light. These new men often have motives that are less than noble—many are trying to garner media interest that will spread their names and advance their careers. In the same way, many of the old guard did what they did out of a true sense of honor. But the final result, it seems, will be a cleaner police force. Whatever the case, it seems clear to me that without a recognition that policemen are human and subject to temptation, and without a policy that provides someone to watch over the individual

activities of the police, the problem of corruption will never
be solved.

So I sit here now and mull over what all this means. But
from time to time other questions pop up in my mind, questions I know are fruitless to ask but which I can't seem to
get out of my head. Why did Tommy change the way he did?
What made Joe turn on us all? You can say drugs, but I'm
not satisfied with the simplicity of that answer. And most importantly, what happened to those six duffel bags full of gold
and jewels? No doubt a lot of dough went into coke. Before
Bucky disappeared he had expanded his business and his connections, and I've already described Joe's affairs in that world.
I'm sure Bucky and Joe also threw away a lot of cash on their
junkets to Las Vegas and Atlantic City. But the biggest spending spree in the world couldn't have exhausted the twenty-
odd million in diamonds and gold Bucky spread over the floor
of Joe's basement. At night I still have dreams of those pink
diamonds, black pearls and sapphire-studded rings. Where did
they go? Are they buried in some distant back yard? Hidden
in a hollowed-out wall? Sitting in some new safety deposit box
in Florida or New York or Switzerland? Maybe Joe Bangs
knows. Maybe the knowledge disappeared with Bucky. I'll
probably never know, and it is probably just as well.

We all got what was coming to us. When Brother, Kenny
and Tommy heard the sentence I got, they couldn't plead guilty
fast enough. All the scheming I had done with Brother and
Kenny during my trial suddenly meant nothing. As Brother
said to me later: "When I heard they gave you thirty to forty, Jerry, I fell through my asshole." He and the others broke
their legs getting to the judge.

Tommy got eighteen to twenty, to be served concurrently
with the time he got for shooting Joe. He has yet to be sentenced for his botched drug deal in Mississippi, so he won't
be out for a long time. Kenny got nine to twelve, so he'll be
eligible for parole two years from now. He is already in a pre-
release program. Brother, as I expected, is philosophical about

the whole affair. He took his twelve-to-fifteen-year sentence with a shrug. He's been there before. Joe is not serving any time, but in a way I see him as being the worst off of all of us. He has to live with his coke habit and his twisted personality, something I wouldn't wish on anyone.

And me? Well, I'm serving my time and doing my homework. The consequences of my life of crime are not over by any means; I am now the chief witness in a federal case regarding those civil service exams I stole. The case promises to blow the lid off an awful lot of police corruption in this state, and before it's over the repercussions will be felt throughout the country. You see, when I started—well, I'm getting ahead of myself again. As I've said before, that's another story.